The Financial Universe

Planning your investments using Astrological Forecasting

To
Saturn

The Financial Universe

Planning your investments using Astrological Forecasting

CHRISTEEN SKINNER

A Guide to
Identifying the
Role of the
Planets and Stars
in World Affairs,
Finance and
Investment

THE Alpha PRESS

BRIGHTON • PORTLAND

2 4 6 8 10 9 7 5 3 1

First published 2004 in Great Britain by
THE ALPHA PRESS
PO Box 2950
Brighton BN2 5SP
UK

British Library Cataloguing in Publication Data
Skinner, Christeen
   Financial Universe
   1. Astrology and business   2. Investments
   I. Title
   133.5'83326

ISBN 1 898595 44 5

Cover image: Geodetic Astrogeography Solar Eclipse, 11 July 2010.

Typeset and designed by G&G Editorial, Brighton.
Printed by MPG Books, Bodmin, Cornwall.
This book is printed on acid-free paper.

Contents

Preface   vi
Acknowledgements   x

1 The Changing Sky   1
2 Stars and Sacred Places   12
3 World Trade and Planet Cycles   17
4 Forecasting   25
5 Transformation   35
6 Collapse of the USA   44
7 The World Bank   60
8 The Credit Bubble and Currency Collapse   71
9 Water Wars, 2010   80
10 Illusions and Imagination   94
11 Cutting Edge   104
12 Wall Street and London Markets, 2004–2020   111

Notes   146
Bibliography   153
Index   157

Preface

This book offers a view of the future from the perspective of the past, and most particularly, the ancient past. The stars and cosmos have always fascinated mankind: analysis of planetary cycles, more commonly called astrology, has been used as a forecasting technique for thousands of years. More recently, a separate branch of this study has evolved – *Financial Astrology*. This branch of astrology combines planet, solar and recognised business cycles. Its use alerts investors to periods, places and circumstances where investment caution needs to be exercised, and to times when opportunities to invest positively are more open and less prone to negative cosmic interference.

Since beginning astrological studies twenty-five years ago, I have been increasingly aware of developing patterns in planetary and other activity within our solar system. Experience has demonstrated specific correlations between planetary activity and trends in social, economic and political behaviour. By analysing the 'state of the solar system' at specific times, and from specific locations, I have identified potential periods of stress for investors, companies and business sectors. In looking ahead over the coming sixteen years, I see patterns developing that give cause for alarm. Detailed astrological analysis of the unfolding patterns within our solar system indicates that the potential for global rifts and difficulties is far greater than that imagined by even the most negative media correspondents and politicians. Cosmic conditions and circumstances in the coming decade have major implications not only for the world economy, but also, perhaps, for the very survival of large sectors of the world's population.

My forecasting expertise to date has centred on the business and financial world. In this, I have been moderately successful. On numerous occasions I have been able to hone in on specific dates as market turning points and have identified sectors of the markets likely to experience growth or pressures. Many of my clients have consulted with me for over a decade, and seek advice on a weekly, sometimes daily, basis. Other clients come for advice only for specific events, such as the launch of a new product. These various individuals and companies find this input useful – especially when used alongside information gleaned from other consultants working in their business sector. Clients have encouraged me to commit my thoughts about the coming twenty years to paper. It is my sincere hope that the understanding of solar and planetary cycles will be helpful to private investors, fund managers, financial advisors and chief executives.

The Financial Universe presents a view of how global stock markets might react to world events between now and 2020. The discussion is broken down into specific time periods, in the context of the future relations between nations, the possibility of global conflict, and the underlying motifs or reasons that might cause severe disruption or discontinuity to the way in which the world works and trades.

This work focuses on the *potential* for massive disruption as a result of specific cosmic circumstances; but, it is only that – *potential*. It is possible, indeed probable, that under the great stresses and strains signalled for the coming period, great good will be achieved – most likely post-2012. History provides evidence that mankind is more than capable of compassionate and innovative behaviour. Those in positions of political, economic and military leadership could take note of the coming cosmic squalls and modify their behaviour accordingly. They could turn out to be truly great leaders. They would, in effect, accept their relative position in the cosmos, and make every effort to work with natural forces rather than against them.

Understanding of our cosmos, the solar system and the cycles of the planets does not, in isolation, hold the only keys to a better way of doing things. But in conjunction with human endeavour, the spiritual quest, and the march of civilization forward, they can be extraordinarily useful. If, as I suggest, there is correlation between the state of the solar system and mankind's behaviour, then understanding this correlation – how we may react at a future time bearing in mind how mankind has reacted to similar conditions in the past – offers us a window on the future. At the very least we need to look through this window in order to prepare for difficulties if not to avoid them.

Since the stock market dramas of 2000, there has been much speculation as to the collective financial future of the West. Savings and pension forecasts concern everybody. Commentators are able to offer guidance in the short-term by identifying the best financial packages on offer at a particular time. They generally express the view that the investor should look to the long-term. They base their financial models on past performance whilst offering the caveat that past performance cannot be guaranteed in the future. Even the best of fund managers recognise that there is an element of risk and that it is beholden on the investor to keep well-informed. *The Financial Universe* offers a rare perspective – one which holds appeal for those willing to look to the skies and beyond.

The chapters that follow open with an assessment of our relationship with the cosmos and the influence of solar activity on life on Earth. Using historical analysis, the chapter on 'World Trade and Planet Cycles' reviews previous periods of financial difficulty and looks ahead to periods when similar patterns will recur. 'Forecasting' considers recent financial dramas – most notably those of April 2000. The following chapter, 'Transformation', considers an outlook fraught with danger. The astrological links, though not absolutely rigid, seem to point to major events that involve massive changes in currency exchange and the potential for global warfare within the next decade.

'The Collapse of the USA', 'The World Bank', 'The Credit Bubble and Currency Collapse' and the 'Water Wars' chapters explain the potential for cataclysmic events with their inevitable impact on the financial world. The seeds of these issues are already apparent. Editorials in daily newspapers are continually making us aware of the potential difficulties that lie ahead. But solutions or meaningful steps that might counter the overwhelming forces that seem to be lining up to cause mayhem and mischief to the financial and trading system of the world, and indeed to the world as we know it today, are rarely offered.

'Illusions and Imagination' sets out to show that by being aware of cosmic energies and planet cycles, the human race will be better able to shape a future towards peace and enlightenment. Clashes cannot be avoided. The violence of the cosmos around us implies these to be natural. Our task is to apply knowledge of the cosmos – knowledge that has been used by mankind from the beginning of human activity on earth – to avoid needless slaughter, extreme hardship and famine.

'Cutting Edge' assesses which industries are most likely to experience positive development in the coming years and which potentially offer investment growth. The concluding chapter, 'Wall Street and London Markets, 2004–2020', appraises various expected cosmic events and suggests their possible influence on the global marketplace. Specific dates are given to mark expected turning points and suggestions are made as to which sectors will benefit during specific periods.

The coming years promise to be active and challenging. Private investors, fund managers, captains of industry and others may find the view of the future offered in this book to be a useful adjunct to information gleaned from other futurologists. They may also find that the specific dates and time-lines mentioned equip them with invaluable foreknowledge. In reflecting on the correlation between historical events and various planetary and star alignments, the reader is encouraged to consider current issues from this ancient perspective and in so doing to consider their own place amongst the stars. It is my earnest hope that reading this book may mark the beginning of a thought-provoking journey. For those interested to know more, a list of further sources for study is offered in the Bibliography.

Although there are several periods in the coming years that appear particularly prone to conflict and financial difficulty, there are other years when the quest for peace and happiness may be realised. This book does not focus just on doom and gloom, booms and busts. The message I wish to impart is one of potential and opportunity.

Acknowledgements

I would like to take this opportunity to thank my many friends, clients and students who have encouraged me over the last three years to complete this work. In particular, I thank Anthony Grahame of The Alpha Press for his support in bringing this publication to fruition. I extend my warm thanks to Mark Ford, Ann Sydney, Chris Oglivie, Claire Underwood, Mike Underwood, John Ware and Dudley Warrington-Thomas for reading the later drafts of the book and for offering gentle guidance – their assistance is much appreciated. The author is indebted to the many computer programmers whose sterling work made the process of researching dates so pleasurable.

Finally, and most importantly, it has been Michael Skinner's understanding and patience that has allowed *The Financial Universe* to evolve to book form. And for this and for other suns, words are not adequate.

The Financial Universe

Planning your investments using
Astrological Forecasting

The Changing Sky

The coming sixteen years promise to be both exciting and challenging. Advances and breakthroughs in technology and medicine will offer solutions to some of the world's greatest problems. Equally, disputes between nations bring the threat of unimaginable disaster to large areas of the world. Imagining our future can be as frightening as it is exhilarating. Forecasting our future may seem impossible – beyond our imagination. Yet, it is possible that we are equipped as never before to face a future that is less uncertain than at any time past. With information available literally at our finger-tips via the Internet, we can explore possibilities that free us from the limits of our personal imagination, and explore whole new worlds.

Prediction is neither an art nor a science. At its extremes it meets art through the interpretation of symbols, as in tarot cards, and meets science in the world of actuaries, physicists and mathematicians. Developments in the fast-changing world of 21st century physics suggest that the range of these extremes may be much narrower than previously thought. There is already recognition that the observer can influence the outcome of an experiment. It would seem that both the time and place – and the individuals present – have an effect. It is even possible that an imagined outcome can be 'made to happen' through the application of thought waves. Today's new science acknowledges the effect that the experimenter has on the experiment itself. Quantifying this is likely to require analysis of the moment and place of an experiment coupled with analysis of those moments and places unique to the individuals involved. The truly detached scientist may need to be some distance from the experiment and to monitor events from afar.

The most important event in our own lives is our arrival on Earth. Our personal history begins on a particular day, at a particular time, and in a particular place — factors that differentiate us from others and make us unique. For some, a family myth surrounds the moment itself. We might, possibly, know that we were born 'just before lunch' or 'in the middle of a thunderstorm'. The factual evidence that is our birth certificate records the date, place and, in many parts of the world, the local time. Photographs show who was present and convey something of our personal social history. Barring interviews with those around at the time, or graphic pictorial evidence, however, there may be no record of the local weather or the sights and sounds outside the actual room of our birth. We may eventually learn that we had a 'difficult start' or an 'easy birth', yet we know little of the collective thinking and pressures of the moment. Knowledge illuminates the time for us. A Birth Date newspaper sets us thinking about the ideas and hopes of the period, whilst relatives regale us with stories of what was happening for them at the time of our arrival.

Of course, the Earth did not actually stop turning while our birth took place. It continued its twenty-four hour axial rotation. Similarly, the Earth continued to move in its path around the Sun. But the Sun — indeed, the whole solar-system — moved too, sweeping through the sky at enormous speed. Within just one hour of our birth we travelled 66,600 miles.[1] It is fascinating to learn whether these were 'bumpy' miles, the universe being a strange and arguably a dangerous place. If we arrive during a period of freak activity we may consider this the norm and therefore be ill at ease during times of calm. It is even possible that we are unable to access our many talents until similar stressful conditions recur.

It has been shown that every human breath contains at least 700,000,000 electrically charged particles.[2] Our very first breath is charged according to the collision of cosmic rays, uranium and thorium emissions from the soil, and atmospheric conditions. The very air that we first breathe, itself affected by the local environment, begins the process of biological mutation that colours the rest of our lives. That air is not static. It too moves according to weather and atmospheric conditions. It is entirely possible that human behaviour is affected thereby — bringing out the worst and best in us at different times, with some people more affected than others. Just as terrestrial weather can yield clues as to patterns of behaviour, so too might solar or cosmic changes.

As children we learn that the Earth circumnavigates the Sun along with the other planets of the solar system. We learn too that our Sun is not particularly special. There are billions upon billions of similar stars in the sky.

This apparent downgrading of the Sun seems unfortunate. It can still our thirst for more knowledge about this star which IS special to us. Without its energy, life on Earth could not be sustained. The ancients worshipped it. Such behaviour may be inappropriate for our apparently more enlightened age, but we could, perhaps, show a little more respect for the condition of the Sun and the system that it dominates.

We know that most of us 'feel good' on sunny days, and arguably this influences our attitudes and behaviour on those days. Knowing even more about the different ways in which the Sun can affect us and, indeed, predicting how it might affect us in the coming twenty years, could be extraordinarily helpful in planning our future. Nor should we stop there. The Sun is not alone in generating energy within our immediate universe. Comets, radio waves from other galaxies, and magnetic storms, generate other forms of energy that have their own effect too. Whilst our personal family myth might record that we were born during a violent storm when the rain lashed at the windows, it probably did not record the external and unseen violence at work beyond the Earth's stratosphere.

What we do know may be limited to the recordings of family photograph albums. History books too are replete with dates of specific events that may have relevance for us. Dates, pictures and photos are powerful mnemonics. Just the dates alone conjure pictures of the epoch, the time of year, and the social, economic and political environment. The local weather conditions on the day are rarely mentioned in text but may be seen in pictorial evidence. For over a century, photographic evidence has helped evoke a period. Earlier, mankind was reliant on the work of artists, who either gathered their information through eye-witness reports, or accepted folklore. These artistic impressions are particularly interesting since some portray events that would tend not to be recorded either by photos or in academic history books.

The Bayeaux Tapestry gives us pictorial evidence of a specific event. We are shown graphic illustration not only of the Battle of Hastings but also of the comet[3] that appeared in the sky at around the same time. The extra-terrestrial event adds a curious and powerful dimension to defining the moment. In the same way that the picture of a battle amid a tempestuous sea reminds us that those involved were coping with two quite different enemies, we might just wonder about cosmic applying forces.

Increased understanding of the path and cycles of eclipses and planets has allowed astronomers to conjecture the cosmological nature of the Star of Bethlehem – now thought to have been a conjunction of the three bright planets, Venus, Jupiter and Saturn, perhaps coupled with a comet. The three 'wise men' are thought to have been sky-watchers or astronomers, whose task included the forecasting of the effect of celestial activity on mankind. More recent sky watchers have offered cosmic events as explanations for the flood mentioned in the myths of ancient cultures. Disturbed planetary behaviour, perhaps caused by asteroid collisions, may have created freak weather conditions on Earth. Similar reasoning is put forward to explain the demise of the dinosaurs.

Occasionally we are reminded that a predictable cosmic event, e.g. a Full Moon, might have been an important factor in choosing a date. Black and white film of World War II frequently shows bombing raids timed to coincide with this lunar phase. For example, the raids now known as 'The Dambusters'[4] were planned to take place over the period of the Full Moon. Like some extraordinary torch-beam, the natural light of the moon focused on a period of unique activity.

Then there is the choice of a moment within the day itself. In days of old, kings were crowned at the moment when the Sun itself crowned the sky – approximately midday local time. This was viewed as a moment of natural brilliance which, it was hoped, would reflect on the new King's reign.

These tantalising glimpses of thought-out choice suggest many links between cosmic or extra-terrestrial activity and the development or action of life on Earth. As the Hubble telescope relays fantastic data back to us and space physicists learn more about the state of our universe generally, the potential to forecast pending changes in cosmic condition increases. It may not be long before the general terrestrial weather forecast is augmented by analysis of the cosmic day ahead.

The Sun

The Sun is inconstant. Given that we need its energy to survive, information about solar energy has dramatic implications. Those studying human cell growth and re-growth, disease, crops, earth studies and more may find this knowledge to be a critical factor in their work. Prediction of solar activity is a science still in its infancy, yet what we know already gives a fairly clear picture as to what to expect in the years ahead and could give us guidance as to when we might consider modifying our reactions, to take account of bizarre conditions.

The Changing Sky

Our Sun, a yellow dwarf star, lies in one of the spiral arms of the Milky Way. It is not particularly special; it joins thousands and thousands of others to revolve around the Galactic Centre, taking 220 million years[5] to complete the journey. It is similar in size and mass to around 10 per cent of the other stars in our galaxy. Like the Earth, it spins on its axis. Unlike the Earth, it does not spin uniformly. It spins faster in the middle than at its poles, with a variation of approximately two earth days[6] between the equatorial and polar-regions. It is inherently unstable and warrants our vigilance on its changing state.

The Sun burns helium to generate both the light and heat needed to sustain life on Earth. However, it does not generate the same amount two days in a row. At times in our pre-history, the light and heat have been obliterated by dust caused by the dramatic impact of meteors or asteroids on the Earth. We know that such events are catastrophic for life. Too much or too little of either light or heat is dangerous for all living creatures. The so-called holes in the ozone layer have already necessitated a change in our attitudes towards certain products and their emissions. Now there is talk of using advanced technology both to detect possible collisions with cosmic rock and to deflect it from the Earth's path. Protecting ourselves from a major incident that might prevent the Sun's powerful rays from reaching us is being given increased attention. Some sort of cosmic defence shield may be necessary before long.

It is, of course, known already that the Earth is hit by cosmic debris of varying size on an almost daily basis. Mostly this debris is broken up within the Earth's atmosphere and, as a result, does minimal harm. Debris of this kind is easy for us to relate to. Less easy to identify are cosmic forces which cannot be seen by the naked eye.

Our local star is also the source of an inconstant stream of gases known as the solar winds. These have an effect on bodies outside the Earth's stratosphere. Satellites orbiting above the Earth are affected by this energy and the lives of these satellites can be shortened by exposure to the radiation carried on these waves. This same solar wind poses a threat to astronauts and causes damage to the Earth's magnetic field. It may be that it affects each and every one of us. Soon it may be shown that our ability to regenerate and to maintain optimum cell structure depends on the magnetic field operating within certain limits. It could be that the mutation of cells, causing cancerous growths, is the result of extreme variation in these fields. Some humans may be more susceptible to fluctuations than others. Magnetic therapy for this group may be just one of the advances made in the coming decade.

The Sun also generates tongues of fire known as solar flares. Typically, a solar flare will generate 10^{27} ergs per second[7] – ten times greater than the energy released from a volcanic explosion. Flares occur when a build-up of magnetic energy in the solar atmosphere is suddenly released. This radiation works across the entire gamut of known wavelengths: from radio waves to gamma rays. The Earth experiences bombardments of these too. Again, we have little understanding of the effect of these but it seems reasonable to suggest that they may have some influence.

As yet, it appears that there is no rhythm to these flares. They are unpredictable. They can be seen though, and since we know how long it takes for sunlight to reach Earth, we can be given warning of the impending arrival of this extra energy. Such information could prove particularly helpful. It might go some way towards explaining why there are sudden outbursts of creativity or malevolence. Study of human activity on the days following a solar flare, and at the time that the extra boost of energy reaches Earth, is tantalising, suggesting as it does that we are affected by these surges. Foreknowledge of their arrival would give us the option of modifying our behaviour. It is not inconceivable that information about these flares could be given alongside information offered to those who suffer when there is increased pollen in the air.

Sunspots |

Observations of the Sun over thousands of years have shown that spots appear on its surface. Some days there may be none, whilst at others times there may be as many as 200 or more. Sunspots are curious. They appear in latitudinal bands about 40 degrees either side of the solar equator. One series begins in the northern hemisphere and works down across the solar equator to a position about 40 degrees latitude, with the next series starting at this southernmost point and moving back up. Differentiating one sunspot or cluster of sunspots from another is not easy. As the Sun spins at different rates with some spots grouping together or merging, confusion arises. Each series takes a little over 11 Earth years. From one north-start series to the next is approximately 22 years. There is, as yet, no general consensus as to what causes sunspots to occur, but there is little doubt that the gravitational pull exerted on the Sun by the planets plays a part.

The presence of a large number of sunspots has several effects. Short-wave radio transmission can be disrupted for days at a time when the

maximum point in the sunspot cycle is reached – a potentially serious difficulty for those travelling at latitude extremes or across the seas.[8]
Disturbances have also been noted in computer technology and in the
performance of orbiting satellites. These disturbances in the sun also affect
radio waves. Those travelling in aircraft at a time of peak sunspot activity
are subjected to the equivalent of an X-ray during their journey. The Earth's
electro-magnetic field too is affected by changes in sunspot number – a fact
that may be of interest to those studying Earth movement, volcanic eruptions and earthquakes.[9]

It is perfectly possible that sunspots affect all of us to a greater or lesser
extent. An interesting piece of medical research showed that in 72 per cent
of 237 cases,[10] a major change in patients' condition occurred on days of
high sunspot activity and when these sunspots were at minimum latitude.
This latter comment is interesting in that it implies that the latitude of the
sunspots within their cycle enhances any effect.

Further study – this time of the New York stock market[11] – suggested
that the fewer the sunspots, the greater people's optimism or lack of willingness to subject positive forecasts to intense scrutiny and common sense.
Thus, years when sunspot activity is at a minimum are commonly bull-
market years. By contrast, the greater the number of sunspots, the more
pessimistic and 'bearish' people become. Knowledge of where we are within
the sunspot cycle looks to have special value for investors.

The actual sunspot activity on any given day varies widely. President
George W. Bush was born on 6 July 1946 during a solar maximum period.
The recorded sunspot activity for that day was 120. By contrast, Prime
Minister Tony Blair was born on 6 May 1953 at the solar minimum. Only
8 sunspots were recorded that day.[12] These facts alone might suggest that
Blair is essentially an optimist. Bush, on the other hand, may be better
attuned to defensive mechanisms on the basis that the worse is yet to come.

Given that the attitude of leaders has a great impact on a nation during
the period of their office, it is interesting to look at the sunspot numbers
applying on the dates of birth of key leaders of the 20th century. Consider
that Margaret Thatcher, Mao Tse Tung and Theodor Roosevelt were all
born, like George W. Bush, within periods of high activity. The situation
was very different for Adolf Hitler (no sunspots) and Churchill (low sunspot
activity). In the case of the latter two, there was an assumption – perhaps
even arrogance – that their vision would be achieved. Perhaps it is the case
that nil or low sunspot activity contributes to clarity of purpose, whilst high
activity allows for plural possibility. This is far too simplistic, of course.

Yet, it may be of interest to look at the activity applying on important dates and to see if it falls within the mean of a period, or is exceptional.

The start of the 21st century has seen a curious phenomenon in the sunspot cycle. The expected peak occurred but, unusually, a 'double top' followed, i.e. sunspots hit a record high, reduced over subsequent days, and then reached that earlier high level once more. Further, in October 2003, two giant sunspots were identified.[13] Solar scientists could not recall a previous occasion when such activity had occurred. Clearly something unusual is occurring, suggesting some disturbance in the natural sunspot rhythm. The 11.2-year cycle moves from low to high and returns to low activity, although the numbers of sunspots do not form a particular pattern. Indeed, the high numbers (200+ per day) recorded in the opening months of the 21st century have not been witnessed since 1980.[14] Had the cycle worked as in the past, the high would have been reached and then there would have been a slow tailing off until the minimum was reached around six years later. The fact that this did not occur might suggest that antici-pated lows will not be reached until a little later – say 2008. From there the phase would move upward again, reaching sunspot highs in 2013/14 and lows at the end of our 20-year period around 2020.

In terms of stock market movement we might conclude a general bullish trend as the sunspot numbers drop, into 2007/8, and a bear-trend period roughly six years later as maximum levels are reached once more. This assumes, of course, that the cycle follows its usual pattern. Any change in the cycle warrants our close attention if we are to draw any conclusions or make investment decisions based on it. The last time the 'double top' phenomenon was observed was in the opening years of the 20th century.[15] A little over a decade later the number of sunspots had tailed off to reach solar minimum in 1914.[16] And that year World War broke out. It is not inconceivable that the same could occur in the early years of this new century. As the number of sunspots falls from this double-peak activity, the potential for hostilities between nations increases. Indeed, this particular perspective on the correlation between aggravated activity on Earth and cosmic tension is just one of several to signal a problematic period at the end of the first decade of the new Millennium.

Some scientists have speculated that the wide variation in the numbers of sunspots occurring at any time is a factor in terrestrial climate change. Between the years 1645 and 1715 (the Maunder Minimum[17]) virtually no sunspots were sighted. However, in any given 30-year period over the past hundred years, 40,000–50,000 sunspots have been recorded.[18] Between

1672 and 1699, the scientist Sporer found less than 50 to have been observed.[19] Some have drawn the conclusion that this lack of activity was a major contributory factor in the colder weather experienced on the Earth throughout that period. Such a period has not recurred – but presumably, could. We know that a solar minimum period is due around 2007. Should this see the start of a prolonged period devoid of sunspots entirely – and this is something we would know quickly – major adjustments in thinking would be necessary. Should such conditions occur, investors in particular might want to take immediate action.

Predicting solar activity is a science still in its infancy. Further studies will need to be undertaken before it can be determined whether or not the solar latitudes at which sunspots occur have a correlation with life on Earth. What is important for the moment is that we are aware of the value of information about solar power – in all its many forms.

Further Thoughts |

One thing we do know for certain is that the motion of the 'wandering stars' or planets of our solar system have an effect on our special star, the 'Sun'. Whilst it is convenient to think of the Sun as being at the centre of our universe, this is not the case. The centre of the solar system is known as the Barycentre – a point in space around which the Sun and its accompanying system of planets rotate.[20] When the largest of the planets come together in a particular grouping they create a special set of circumstances where the interconnecting gravitational pull is such that the Sun appears to rotate backwards *against* the Barycentre.

Such an event happens rarely – just seven times in the last 3400 years.[21] Many generations do not experience the effect at all. Those who do, enjoy an accelerated rate of social change, as is well expressed in the most recent solar variation of this kind. The Sun came to this critical point in relation to the Barycentre in 1989/90 – a time of extraordinary events on Earth.

Social change on a grand scale was vividly illustrated by the fall of the Berlin Wall, which brought in its wake talk of the collapse of communism and the death of a particular ideology. Sweeping political upheavals also saw the outbreak of war in many areas – most noticeably in the Balkans.

That same period saw the beginning of extraordinary disruption in the Earth's usual weather patters. We have now seen fires in Indonesia, Australia and America, the result of particularly dry weather; floods across

Europe and central Asia; and ferocious winters in parts of America and across northern parts of the old Soviet Union. Such dramatic change in weather patterns is not unusual in the years following this solar variation. As is common in the first decade following this solar event, a refugee crisis began. Whatever the social, economic, political or climatic reasons that drove people to move from one place to another, the fact is that moving populations have brought with them particular difficulties.

This is not so dissimilar to the years 1632–1633 and 1810–1812, when the Sun was affected in this way before.[22] The former period witnessed extraordinarily cold weather. Indeed, paintings show the Frost Fair held on a frozen River Thames. In the fifteen years following the 1810–1812 solar phenomenon, Europe experienced an entire year of winters. One can only imagine the accompanying hunger as populations sought to feed themselves. Not much later, Napoleon's army was forced back from the Russian front by appalling weather conditions for which they were ill-prepared. In each of these three cases – following 1989, 1810 and 1632 – significant political and social change was experienced. The pace of social, economic and political change accelerated.

The solar disturbances of the 17th and 19th centuries seem to have taken between 15 and 20 years to peter out. Disturbed terrestrial weather patterns do settle down and there is, perhaps, less need for sections of the world's population to migrate in search of better conditions. If this pattern repeats, then the present refugee crisis affecting so many different parts of the world, may well abate after 2005. Certainly, politicians across the world will have put regulations in place so as to make such movement more difficult.

Using our 'start' date of April 1989, it seems probable that it could take until 2009 for populations to stabilise. Politicians meanwhile, driven by the need to 'do something' about the world's refugee crisis and the international trading difficulties caused by friction between nations, could arrive at the conclusion that a new global forum – superseding the present United Nations – will be necessary. As we shall see later, there are reasons to think that such a body would be inaugurated towards the end of 2006. Arriving at this conclusion requires understanding of the role of the planets as they orbit the Sun. Later, through analysis of their historic orbits, we shall see how such a forecast can be made.

In recent years climate change has been recognised and much has been written about the social and economic changes that will be inevitable consequences of new developments in terrestrial weather patterns. Cosmic weather is no less important. As we learn more about the condition of the

Sun and gain knowledge of the links between the position of the planets as they encircle our life-giving star, so it becomes possible to forecast political, social and economic movements with a continually improving degree of probability and accuracy.

Our Financial Universe need not be a mystery. Correlation between the number of sunspots and global economic activity suggests an increase in stock market indices values as sunspot numbers diminish. We may expect that those born on days when there was minimal solar activity will seize the initiative during the coming solar minimum period and probably make gains. This, after all, will be similar solar energy to that which surrounded them at their most important moment — their arrival on Earth. Equally, those born during a time of high sunspot activity may be cautioned that at the solar minimum their judgment may be deficient. It is important to stress the word 'may'. By definition individuals vary. A simple test of judgment is possible, however. The sunspot number on your day of birth can be accessed via the Internet.[23] Noting this and similarly noting the solar activity on earlier days when you made important financial decisions provides greater self-understanding of the influence of solar weather on personal judgment. The more we know about our actions in relation to cosmic activity the better we may monitor our financial behaviour.

Stars and Sacred Places

ur Sun may be our nearest star and may have great influence on life on Earth, but it is not the only star to have import for us. The ancients understood this well, as can be shown by the positioning of pyramids and monoliths that are aligned with the constellations.

The positioning of these various buildings would seem to form part of a language that has long been forgotten but which was clearly based on geometric principles that correlated terrestrial features with cosmic co-ordinates. Satellite pictures showing grid-forms over South America, in particular, suggest superior intellects who planned and created sophisticated structures. Whether these intellects were native to the Earth we cannot know. What is clear is that mankind's fascination with the heavens stretches over millennia and may be rooted in dialogue with beings that had far a far more profound understanding of time and space than is held at present.

Were it not for our Sun, the only light available on Earth would come from the stars – and we would see stars for twenty-four hours of every day. We cannot do this because daylight interferes. We have to await nightfall for the stars to become visible. It is curious watching these lights appear. The brightest stars appear first but are soon joined by hundreds and thousands of others. Some appear fixed high above us. Other stars apparently rise and set as the Earth rotates. Which stars come into our view depends on our particular latitude, with the greatest variation being between people living either side of the terrestrial equator, for instance those in the northern hemisphere have a view of the Big Dipper or Plough, whilst those in the south are familiar with the Southern Cross. Neither formation is visible from the 'wrong' side of the equator.

The situation is further complicated by another slow rotation. As the solar system travels through space the constellations appear to fly by too. To see tonight's star performances replicated exactly, will require you to live for 26,000 years[1] – the time it takes for the constellations to revolve on their axis. A reference point is useful. For the last thousand or so years, the star named Polaris – at 680 light years'[2] distance from us – has been designated our Pole Star since it lies at approximately 90 degrees from the ecliptic (the word used to describe the Sun's apparent path around the Earth). Indeed, as the Earth itself rotates, it appears that the constellations are rotating around this point.

A few thousand years ago Polaris did not hold this northerly axis. It has taken thousands of years for it to move into this place and it will be further thousands before it slips back to a point in the south. In fact, even now, Polaris is still some way off mathematical exactitude with the actual pole. It will reach this point around AD 2102.[3] Polaris will then slowly slip away and, eventually, another star will take its place at this northerly point. It will then be another 26,000 years before Polaris becomes our North Pole star once more.

Some astrological tomes refer to the twinkling objects of the night sky as 'fixed stars'. They are only fixed in the sense that they appear to hold a position for many, many years relative to the Earth's cycle. Astronomers, however, recognise that their position does change. The famous star maps created by Norton[4] are redrawn every 50 years to reflect this movement. Over hundreds of years, the position of stellar bodies changes dramatically. As we have noted, the star we term the Pole or 'North Star', Polaris, was not the pole star of some thousands of years ago, and in less than a century it will start to slip from this role once more.

The effect, then, of this long, slow cycle results in different stars and constellations being visible to varying groups of people. Bronze Age Man would have enjoyed a sky picture very different from that seen by Renaissance Man, for example, whilst Prehistoric Man would have sought meaning in a sky littered with star shapes very different to those that we witness today.

As we know, the stars are not equidistant from us. We know too that the sun, or nuclear orb of gas, that made them a star may no longer be burning. Light from stars may take many years to reach us. If we could cross that time-span we might find that there is now no matter left where once the star shone brightly. The idea that the stars can actually influence life on Earth becomes an even more bizarre concept when we concede that not only are stars too far away to affect us in any meaningful way, but they may not, in fact, be there at all! Such knowledge renders it all too easy to dismiss the changing sky as an irrelevance.

Yet there is a seductive case for accepting that human beings' relationship with viewable stars has pertinence. This could have more than a little to with our understanding of perception. Our eyes complete a whole host of tasks in order for us to understand the world around us. Not only do they identify an object, they evaluate the strength of that object and that object's frame of reference. Our eyes analyse perspective to determine just how near or far the object is from us – and whether or not the object is travelling towards us or away from us. The stars, though, remain a mystery. Viewed with the naked eye they give little clue as to their size, or even their actual position. We can, however, form some idea as to their magnitude according to their brightness. Thus it is that since time immemorial some stars have gained 'super-star' status – and a mythology to match.

Stars and Their Influence

Certain stars – visible with the naked eye – have acquired particular reputations. Some are deemed fortunate and positive whilst others have decidedly negative associations. The associations used were based on qualities attributed to the wandering stars – or planets. So, any particular star could be said to be 'of the nature of planet beta and planet gamma'. The myths associated with the planets were thus adopted to describe the attributes of the more permanent stars. How and why the stars have acquired particular reputations has, to a large extent, been lost in the mists of time. Nevertheless, the legacy of this thinking would seem to play an important role even today.

The ancients saw Polaris's influence as being 'a mix of Saturn with Venus'.[5] Lacking the benefits of the technology of the telescope, they could only see the planets Mercury, Venus, Mars, Jupiter and Saturn, and used ideas associated with the movements of each of these planets to describe the nature of the stars themselves. They would have noted that Saturn moves slowly around the sky (taking nearly thirty years to complete its journey) and that it appeared to be dimmer than, say, Jupiter or Mars. Because it appeared to have an effect for long periods, they assumed a connection to objects that stand the test of time, and to weighty affairs of state. Venus, the beautiful planet that hangs low in the sky, was seen as something of a siren – a 'look at me' planet.

The people of long ago saw Polaris as a star to relate to (Venus), whose influence would be enduring (Saturn). Modern astrology would suggest that a mix of Saturn and Venus would correlate with difficult relationships, responsibility to others, and inheritances that are tinged with difficulty.

If this association with Polaris has had an influence over the past thousands of years we could, loosely, arrive at a parallel with mankind's struggle to achieve the art of sharing our planet with others and living with the legacies of earlier generations who failed to understand one another. Perhaps by the time Polaris is no longer the Pole Star, humankind will not find it necessary to fight over particular geographic regions or ways of living. Perhaps, when Polaris's position is taken by a more friendly-natured star we will eventually become one Earth-nation. This, though, is unlikely to happen in the next twenty years!

The concept of stellar influence is clearly not new, but it has changed dramatically over the years. Since the discovery of Uranus in 1781,[6] there has been an option to associate the nature of stars with new and revolutionary concepts (traits associated with that planet). Whereas before, stars were attributed with the nature of, say Venus and Saturn, latter day astrologers have been able to note traits associated with Uranus: namely revolution and change. The discovery of Neptune and Pluto has led to even more connotations becoming possible – assuming, of course, that there really *is* correlation between the nature of the stars and the planets orbiting the Sun with us. The simple test must surely be to take any event in history and to see which stars were prominent at that time and in that location, and whether or not the traits associated with prominent stars aligned with specific places at those times were indeed at work.

The presence of a comet at around the time of the Battle of Hastings on the fields of Pevensey was previously noted. In recording the comet, those artists and recorders would also have been noting its transit relative to the constellations in view at that time. The visible stars that day were not the same as those seen in today's evening sky at Pevensey. Those stars are now somewhere between 20 and 30 degrees from their earlier positions. A rough and ready reckoning suggests that each star 'moves' around 8 minutes of arc every 10 years – or around one and a half degrees every 100 years.[7].

On the eve of the Battle of Hastings almost a thousand years ago, as the man who became known as William the Conqueror looked up at the night sky, Polaris would have been some distance from true North. Still, Polaris offered a northerly frame of reference. More interesting than the Pole Star, around which all the other planets appear to rotate, is the positioning of other stars as viewed from that spot. Pevensey lies at 50 degrees and 46 minutes north and at a longitude of zero degrees and 15 minutes east.[8] At nightfall on 13 October 1066, as the stars came into view, it was perhaps the star Formalhaut that caught William's attention. This star was rising on the south-eastern horizon.[9] It is one of the brighter stars and has a reddish tinge. It was said to be of the nature of 'Mercury and Venus' and, according to the ancients, spoke of success, power and good fortune; yet there was also a suggestion of possible malevolence.[10] One scholar suggested that at a certain position it would give an 'immortal' name. Had William had an astrologer with him, no doubt he would have been informed that the presence of this star was a good omen – even if King Harold was being given similar advice from *his* astrologer. Today that same star is visible over Pevensey, but is not the first to appear after sunset. When it does appear it is significantly higher in the sky. The stars that appear on the horizon, or directly overhead at sunset, were deemed by astrologers of long ago to carry special authority.

Though it could not be seen in daylight, astronomers would have known that the star Ascella[11] would not be far from the Sun in the sky at the time of William's coronation. This star is associated with wealth and success and even its unseen presence in the sky above Winchester would have been thought a good omen for the new kingdom.

It is interesting for us to assess which of the myriad stars above us will hold prominence over various capitals of the world in the next twenty years – and which, appearing close to the 'wandering stars' or planets – will hold sway. There is a precedent for doing this. In 1945, at precisely the latitude of Hiroshima and Nagasaki, the planet Pluto, which we will later see to be associated with death and destruction as well as regeneration and power, was rising together with the 'Dog Star', Sirius.[12]

Sirius is the brightest of all the stars in the heavens and has an awesome reputation. Esoteric works describe it as 'the Mundane becoming Sacred'.[13] The suggestion is that any act or event associated with it takes on special and more profound meaning than could ever be contemplated at the time of the action. The awesome devastation at both Hiroshima and Nagasaki can never be forgotten. It is entirely possible that the sacrifice exacted from the Japanese nation will act as a caution and a brake to other administrations tempted to use these particular weapons of mass destruction. As we shall see later, however, there may be great temptation to use these weapons during a difficult period between 2009 and 2010.

World Trade and Planet Cycles

olar and stellar rhythms cannot be considered in isolation despite their impact on life on earth. As they circumnavigate the Sun, the planets too exert their own particular pull on both our local star (the Sun) and the Earth itself. There are symbiotic links between all of these bodies. The Sun is affected by the relative positions of the planets as they travel around it, and the Earth is affected by its satellite the Moon. We know, too, that the link between Sun, Moon and Earth has profound effects.

In considering the future, we can assess specific cycles and their relevance, if any, to our social and economic history. There is considerable discussion as to whether or not there are any more planets orbiting the Sun. The orbit of any planet further away from the Sun than Pluto would clearly be in excess of the approximately 248.5 years[1] that it takes Pluto to encircle our local star. For now, then, the longest cycle between any two planets is that between Neptune and Pluto – the two planets at the edge of our known solar system. These two planets appear in the same area of the zodiac every half-millennium. Closer to the Sun and therefore moving round it faster than Pluto, Neptune moves on past Pluto, taking approximately 492 years[2] to meet up with it once more – a few degrees further forward in the zodiac.[3] The last time they were viewed close together was in the early 1890s.[4]

This cycle correlates with significant cultural shifts from East to West and back again across millennia. If we were to say that between 1398[5] (a previous conjunction) and 1892 (the most recent), the West was the dominant hemisphere, we would now have to look for evidence of a shift towards Eastern values in this, still early, phase of the new cycle that began just over a century ago. The burgeoning influence of certain Eastern religions would seem to support this theory. Similarly, in cultural terms, the West is giving ever-greater credence to the business and artistic styles of the East. From a purely economic vantage, we see evidence of the West selling more and more of its goods to the East, and of the great importance of emerging markets, including China, India and Indonesia.

Such change does not happen overnight, but the slow pace of change does not negate the impact. What emerges may seem a revelation to some, yet will be considered quite normal and routine to others.

Images assist. We may imagine the God of the Sea (Neptune) interacting with the God of the Underworld (Pluto) in dark springs deep below the Earth's surface. When the pressure reaches a certain point, geysers force their way through the Earth's crust, bringing with them confirmation of the activity that has been developing unseen beneath us.

In the early stages of the cycle, evidence of activity is limited. It may take a quarter of the cycle – over a century and a half, in this instance – for our metaphorical geyser to become an accepted part of the landscape. As the most recent Neptune–Pluto cycle began in 1892, it reaches its quarter-cycle phase around 2061.[6] Over the next twenty years, then, we should see growing evidence of these 'geysers' appear in the East, replacing those that burst forth during the 'Western' cycle of 1398–1892. After 2020 we could expect that growth to accelerate.

It is helpful to remember that each succeeding cycle starts in a different area of the zodiac belt. As these cycles begin just a few degrees further along each time, and because the twelve signs of the tropical zodiac are spaced equally across 360 degrees, it becomes clear that a short series of cycles will take place under one sign of the zodiac. These few cycles together represent the better part of three thousand years. To add to our considerations, we must view the apparent half-millennium cultural shift as the smaller unit of a much longer phase.

The 1892 conjunction occurred at 8 degrees of Gemini,[7] whilst the preceding one took place at around 3 degrees of Gemini[8] in 1398. The conjunctions for three thousand years prior to the end of the 15th century had all occurred in the Taurus section of the tropical zodiac.[9] The Gemini phase of this planet pairing is even now in its infancy. The series centred on the next sign, Cancer, will not begin until the year AD 5339.[10] New themes and ideas correlating with traits associated with the various zodiac signs surface, creating a shift in priorities. The earlier 3000-year phase of the Taurus cycle that preceded the present Gemini one could be described as an agrarian age.

The Gemini phase of this cycle would be expected to affect all affairs associated with that sign. Gemini is the first of the Air signs of the zodiac and is principally associated with communication or the dissemination of information. We can learn much about this sign by its influence within the human body. The nervous system is viewed as Gemini in nature. When an outside force has an impact on the body it sends ripples along interconnecting nerves until the whole entity throbs with reaction. We may touch an item and later show an allergic reaction in a quite different part of the body. Information received in one place can have authority in an entirely different area.

Just a century after this cycle began, Columbus was returning to the Old World with news of the New World across the ocean. The impact of one on the other cannot be over-estimated. In truly Gemini form, a free flow of activity from one to the other and back again gave rise to great social and economic change. In terms of commerce, the opening up of the New World had enormous implications. Of course trade had existed for millennia and of course markets are susceptible to the influence of many factors. Astro-economists take into account at least a dozen cycles. Even so, it is curious to note that the concept of the 'company' did not develop until the 16th century as the first of the Gemini Neptune–Pluto cycles took effect.

The idea of sharing information for profit – and risk – in areas of commerce where one did not necessarily have direct expertise gathered momentum from this time. The merchants of the 16th century, meeting in the first coffee-houses, underwrote the cost of expeditions to the Americas for a share in the profits on the products that would be sold on the ship's return. Initially they did not even know what these products might be. Nor did they know the exact dates when the ships would return laden, they hoped, with cargo. Their commercial lives were filled with intrigue, mystery, subterfuge and enticing promise. The traders could not be sure that their investment would be returned at all, yet they accepted the risks and enjoyed the bounty when all went well.

News – the consolidation of information from all four points of the compass – gained value. Rumour-mongering and gossip could and did affect prices. Gemini is, of course, about the dissemination of news of interest but does not vouchsafe its quality. (It is fascinating to note that the art of printing, a skill that enabled thousands to gain knowledge otherwise unavailable, gathered momentum as Pluto first moved into the sign of Gemini, a little ahead of the planet's meeting with Neptune in that sign.) Since 1398, the credence of news sources has been of paramount interest to traders. Misinformation can cause misery, whilst accurate information can bring reward.

World Trade and Planet Cycles

The coffee-house traders of the 15th century have now been replaced by stock market traders and augmented by day traders who buy and sell across continents and in marketplaces they may never actually visit. These small traders, alongside thousands of others, hold equity in companies offering products and services that they might never have occasion to use themselves. They are ultimate traders in the sense that they may not even know anyone who would use these products or services – yet they believe that someone, somewhere, will, and that their shares will bring reward. Their speculation is based on information gleaned from a variety of Gemini-type sources.

Over the centuries, the number of individuals able to share in the risk of new areas of commerce has increased. Indeed, by the time that our second Gemini-rooted, Neptune–Pluto cycle got underway in the late 19th century it was fast becoming apparent that anyone with the cash, and the desire, could take part in this form of commercial speculation. Today those numbers have increased exponentially. Now, the hustle and bustle of the trading floors is giving way to the transfer of information through that most nebulous of media – the Internet. There are now scores of individuals using personal computers to trade. Each acts as a miniature nerve cell within the body of global trading.

They may be unseen, but these individuals are already acknowledged as affecting world commerce for good or ill. Knowledge of local companies, shared with like-minded colleagues across the world, allows small firms to come to prominence quickly. These 'deep-water springs' are found across the surface of the globe. The advent of space satellites and infra-red technology results in all types of information, good and bad, being passed around the world in the space of a few seconds. Even at lonely spots on the planet it is possible for people to communicate with the nerve centres of commercial activity in the capitals of the world and to obtain local knowledge of orders and staff changes within businesses – news of either of which can affect share prices. However, there is as much potential for corruption through misinformation as there is potential for greater comprehension of value, and shared respect.

Just occasionally it is possible to identify particular moments when corruption and even industrial sabotage will take centre stage. Analysis of the first 'Gemini' cycle shows that there were times between 1398 and 1892 when trade took on a less-than-wholesome hue, and times when it changed beyond recognition – occasionally with both aspects of commercial change occurring together. What took place during these periods has left a lasting legacy in both society and politics.

Crisis points occur when any two planets appear at right-angles or in opposition to one another. Thus there are three significant crisis points within any cycle. In the case of our first Neptune–Pluto/Gemini cycle, the first of these occurred between 1568 and 1572.[11] It was during these years that the large-scale trafficking of black slaves began between Sierra Leone and Brazil.[12] During that same period, slave ships returning from Brazil brought maize and sweet potatoes, peanuts and beans to supplement Africa's few subsistence crops.[13] Meanwhile, in Japan, Nagasaki developed as a major port for foreign commerce,[14] opening up new commercial possibilities, while back in the United Kingdom, the Royal Exchange opened in London[15] and offered a prototype department store by renting stalls to retail merchants.

At the half-way point of the cycle, between 1644 and 1648,[16] the number of slaves imported into the Americas advanced to 10,000 per year.[17] These slaves would be set to work in the Brazilian sugar plantations. Meanwhile, following a shipwreck, Dutch traders returned to Holland and urged the need to establish a settlement at Table Bay,[18] at the tip of Africa. This settlement would provision trading ships from the East Indies with fresh fruit and vegetables and, over time, become a major trading station. Trading across the world was changing dramatically.

In 1816,[19] when Neptune and Pluto were once again at right-angles to one another, reorganisation in international trade became apparent once more. The fledgling America decided to levy a tax on imports so as to encourage its young industries.[20] This would eventually lead to whole new systems of controls and trading agreements. The two planets were still in this right-angle formation in 1819 as new methods for preserving foods developed. In New York, salmon and oysters were packed in tins,[22] enabling them to be brought to the tables of those who would otherwise never experience these tastes. Just as exciting was the development of the first eating chocolate by a company in Switzerland[23] – most assuredly opening up new commercial opportunities.

Other phases of this cycle are relevant too. In 1594, when the two planets were just a third of the way through their cycle,[23] the people of Lisbon closed their spice market to the English and Dutch.[24] This led the Dutch and English to trade directly with the Orient, and gave birth to the British and Dutch East India companies.[25]

Between 1704 and 1741,[26] and again between 1776 and 1786,[27] the two planets once again were one-third of a cycle apart. (As viewed from Earth, there are times when the planets can appear to be moving backwards relative to Earth. The slow-moving nature of the two planets in question results in an aspect 'holding' in the sky for long periods – in this case, almost a century.) Extraordinary growth in commercial activity took place in the 18th century, further sowing the seeds of a vibrant international trade that would have been beyond the imagination of those early 14th century traders.

There is a correlation between development in trade and this long cycle. On the one hand, we see great, positive developments. On the other hand, there is ample evidence of the chaos that ensues when trade based on misinformation or deliberate corruption affects the mass market. It was during this first Gemini cycle that the first fault lines in trading activity occurred.

The market crashes variously named 'Tulipmania' and the 'South Sea Bubble' are illustrations of the fragility of long-distance trade. Where once merchants – by definition, professional traders – shared educated trading risks mainly on a face-to-face basis, a century later it was possible for the layman to take part in speculative activity. The potential for these individuals to be misled grew, the more they invested in areas of which they had little real knowledge. The speculation over tulip bulbs that entrapped many, in Amsterdam and elsewhere, is a classic example of the loss that can befall those with insufficient understanding of the marketplace.

Lessons learnt from 'Tulipmania' were cast to one side a few generations later when even kings and courtiers, who might have been assumed to have access to the best information sources, lost heavily in the scandal now known as the South Sea Bubble. Feeding on the ignorance of many, it was possible for unscrupulous traders to stoke the imagination of those who could be seduced into parting with savings in the hope of experiencing untold wealth. Even this event was pushed to the recesses of the collective memory when tantalising new investment opportunities became available.

Whereas once it was merchant ships that opened fresh trading channels, it was to be the railways that would open up vast tracts of country in America and elsewhere. These tracks made way for faster methods of distributing goods and services. Investing in the railroad companies offered an exciting opportunity. The sums of money needed to expand the system were vast, however, and so the merchants who met under the Buttonwood Tree – later to mark the start of Wall Street – recognised that many would have to be encouraged to invest. Presidents of the United States were not immune to the temptation of these investment opportunities. Neither were they immune to great loss when costs rose and returns and profits proved elusive.

Few lessons had been learnt by the time of the dawn of the second cycle.

Indeed, by the end of the 19th century financial services had been added to the list of products on offer. The Barings crisis of 1896[28] was to prove the forerunner of a different type of collapse. (Interestingly, the rescued Barings of this period came into being on a day[29] when both Neptune and Pluto formed part of a dynamic configuration, highlighting the potential for future difficulties when these points were stressfully aligned.) Nor was this to be the last crisis of its kind.

The concept of 'boom and bust', which became part of economic language within the first of the Neptune–Pluto/Gemini cycles, has been developed further during the second cycle. Such events are now a regular feature of the economic landscape. They cannot be predicted through analysis of the patterns created by Neptune and Pluto alone. Even so, the key stages of this cycle determine periods when large numbers of investors might be seduced by grand ideas that have insufficient substance to deliver on their promises.

A rhythm in these 'booms and busts' has evolved in recent times. Few can predict when they will occur, but most agree that the pattern is now ingrained and has become a recognisable feature of economic life. Finance ministers across the world work hard to break this pattern yet still it continues. It may even be said that some economists feel this rhythm to be inescapable. Certainly, for the latter half of the 20th century, that has appeared to be the case.

This same period has witnessed Neptune and Pluto sharing a cosmic dance that places them at around 60 degrees apart from each other. Although events occur at every stage of any cycle, there is general agreement that this phase is not acutely dramatic by itself. It could be argued that with this cosmic pattern, complacency occurs.

The same is not true of those occasions when the two planets are one-eighth of a cycle apart. This is not altogether surprising. It is recognised that at the square and opposition (quarter and half-way) points, there are noticeably marked changes of commercial expression. The semi-square might be expected to have a similar impact. This aspect formed in the 1930s[30] and history may yet show it to be an important unit in the cosmic signature for economic depression. As is the case with every phase in every cycle, there is a legacy for subsequent generations. Creative accountancy has been derided in recent times. Yet it is interesting that those who employed this talent first were either born during the Great Depression, or were taught economics by those who were.

This particular angle will not occur during the coming twenty years.

23

However, between 2037 and 2042[31] Neptune and Pluto will be three-eighths of a circle apart from one another. If there is similar resonance with the period when the two planets were an eighth of a circle apart (the early 1930s), then this period could prove financially fraught for many. Those born during the 1960s can reasonably expect to be alive in 2037 and so could experience this pressure at first hand. During the coming twenty years they may well be saving at a bank, if not directly contributing to a pension fund. Their savings will be entrusted directly or indirectly to fund managers for further investment. Even these experts may not be able to save them from the financial perils that lie ahead. However they protect their accruing wealth, it could be that they will endure a depression in the closing years of their lives. The age at which people become eligible to receive a state pension might well rise in the coming years, but those reaching 65 in 2037 might well benefit from knowing that the year 2037 could be the start of a seven-year period of commercial anxiety and depression. It would arguably be wise for all those who think they may be alive then to prepare for a difficult few years.

If such forecasts can be made through the study of two of the outer planets alone, how much more can be gleaned by incorporating the cycles of the faster moving planets – not to mention such daily information about solar activity as is now widely available from a number of sources?

Forecasting

In May 2000, the known planets of our solar system formed an unusual pattern. As viewed from Earth, a clear formation could be seen: one large group of planets lay at right angles to another, smaller group. Some felt that this unusual line-up would disturb the Earth's geomagnetic field, causing earthquakes, volcanic eruptions and tidal waves. Lloyds of London even offered insurance cover for this possibility.[1] Disturbance did indeed occur. It was not physical, however, but took place across global markets.

The marketplace, by definition, is a place where individuals meet to trade. The mood of those individuals dictates activity in stock markets around the world. Coinciding with this planetary formation, the collective mood turned negative. The value of some stocks, particularly those in the technical sector, fell dramatically. *This had been forecast* using astro-economic techniques. Astro-economists had formed the conclusion that individuals might react to the unusual alignment by reversing their positions and opinions, creating the potential for severe turbulence in equity trading.

Traders rely on information from a variety of sources to assist them in their decision making. Those using the study of planet cycles as part of their investment strategy were at a distinct advantage as the 20th century drew to a close. By asking astro-economists to identify both the time-scale of this potential reversal, and which, if any, stocks might be most affected, they were able to pull out of certain sectors way ahead of the Spring 2000 débâcle.

The astro-economists' theory was based on study of the distances and angles between several of the outer planets. Comparing these with market activity during similar planet alignments in the past brought them to the conclusion that difficult times lay ahead. Of particular interest in their study were the positions of the two planets Uranus and Neptune. These two planets had formed a conjunction in the early 1990s,[2] repeating a 179-year cycle. This particular cycle resonates with other long-term, economic and political cycles and would be likely to have a considerable effect on commerce. Whilst astro-economists of earlier years had not forecast the birth of the 'dot-coms', they had certainly alerted clients to new business developments meeting particular criteria that they felt would mirror the symbolism of this cosmic activity. Arriving at this conclusion did not take them long.

Industries tend to be sensitive to the movements of certain planets, with the symbolism associated with any one planet linking it to certain types of industrial activity, commodities and commercial thinking. Uranus is usually prominently positioned at times of leaps in scientific thought. It is, therefore, linked to advanced technology concepts. The position of Uranus within the zodiac (i.e., in which tropical zodiac sign it is travelling) yields clues as to which industries will be described as making advances that are 'cutting edge'.

Neptune is associated with anything that cannot be contained or is hard to quantify: the shipping industry, virtually anything to do with the sea or water, the drugs industry, media, and insurance. As the concept of the Internet became reality, astrologers were already beginning to attribute this area of commercial development to Neptune and its associated sign, Pisces. The reasoning behind this was simple: the Internet takes no account of physical borders. Information can be disseminated across the world and stored on unknown computers owned by unknown people in areas of the world alien to those furnishing the information. The effect of this is hard to quantify, as are the effects of marketing campaigns (another Neptune industry).

The linking of Uranus (ever-faster technology) with the concept of the Internet promised to be a heady mix and one that would revolutionise business practices. Similar commercial drama had occurred at a previous conjunction in 1821.[3] At that time it was steam (Neptune) technology (Uranus) that gave birth to the steam engine. This earlier technological revolution led to the advent of railways which subsequently opened up thousands of new trading opportunities with far-reaching effects. These were the 'dot-com' companies of the 19th century. For the astro-economist, comparing the rise and fall of the railways and ancillary industries with the Uranus–Neptune cycle proved exciting..There was a clear correlation. It required no great leap of imagination then to infer that the age of the 'dot-coms' might prove just as exciting, volatile and, for the investor, tremulous.

Indeed, the composition of the *first* Dow Jones index,[4] made up of the top thirty trading stocks in the United States, shows several railway-related industries to have been the high fliers of the first half of the 19th century – just as Microsoft, Cisco and Apple were to become in the early stages of this most recent of Uranus–Neptune cycles. The entrepreneurs of the earlier period were able to capitalise on the technical advances of the time. These stocks were volatile. Those investing in enterprises linked to this new technology embarked on a high-risk strategy. The rewards could be huge. Losses cost even the most eminent of men their savings, however. Former President Ulysses S. Grant was almost bankrupted by investing in rail stocks[5] and he was not alone. Earlier historic falls on Wall Street, and particularly of the stocks associated with the railroads that led in and out of New York Central Station, were every bit as dramatic as the fall of Enron and Worldcom in 2002.

The commercial explosion and technological revolution of the 1990s was comparable to those earlier times. The young 'dot-com' companies pushed forward the Internet as a medium for the distribution of products and services. As with the earlier railroad experiences, these 'dot-coms' suffered difficulties in their first years of trading. Railroad stock blighted many an investor's fortune for the better part of a century. In the early years of the 21st century, it appears to be the turn of the Internet and telecommunications stocks to do the same. The astro-economist, comparing the earlier cycle with the present one, might have drawn the conclusion that the techno-bubble would burst, and so would have been on the look-out for periods when the Uranus–Neptune cycle would become entangled with other cycles. Homing in on the April–May period of 2000 was not difficult. Astro-economists were not alone in suspecting that trouble lay ahead.

Market Drama

Economists, studying business cycles of their own, also felt that market drama might be on the horizon. A major difference between the cycles studied at most business schools and those of the astro-economist is that these business cycles (Juglar, Elliott, Krondatieff etc.) tend to be more fluid. Thus, the beginning and ending of any particular cycle may be confused, and understood better with hindsight. Astro-economists, using the known speeds and distances of the planets, are able to be more specific about the dates when action is likely to occur. Their predictions border on the dramatic, and on this occasion were especially so.

Some City business people are willing to recognise potential parallels between known economic cycles and the orbits of the planets. Many are aware of the Jupiter–Saturn cycle. These two planets meet every twenty years or so and have a marked rhythm that may correlate with a double Juglar cycle.[6] This nine-to eleven-year cycle represents just half of the Jupiter–Saturn 20-year synodic cycle. The natural ebb and flow of business dealings could be explained by the singular planet cycle or the double Juglar cycle. Business people, together with the astro-economists, wondered if the pending Jupiter–Saturn conjunction due in late May 2000[7] might act as a trigger for a denouement in some of the very fast moving sectors. Many individuals were aware of an abnormal peak in sunspot activity and were beginning to form the opinion that extraordinary activity within the solar system could yield extraordinary activity in the marketplace. Few, though, were quite ready to accept the potential for spectacular collapse as forecast by astro-economic colleagues.

Astro-economists had given particular attention to the Jupiter–Saturn conjunction of May 2000, since it would be the last to occur in an Earth sign for many, many years. They suspected that words such as 'savings' and 'prudence' and 'controlled spending' would become the buzz-words of politicians and bankers world-wide. As it became apparent that even the most conservative estimate showed world debt levels to be in the high trillions of dollars, astro-economists wondered if a spectacular fall in stocks might be just the first of an avalanche of financial disasters. They felt that individuals and industries with little experience of the overall business cycle, and of the booms and busts experienced in earlier times, were about to be brought to earth figuratively with a bang. The 'yuppies' of the 1980s, the baby dot-commers and those who had speculated widely on the young technological industries – and the NASDAQ – would experience personal financial earthquakes.

Attitudes to money and business had changed dramatically in the last quarter of the 20th century. Young entrepreneurs, the 'yuppies' of the 1980s, could buy and sell using non-tangible assets. A new term, 'derivatives', entered the traders' vocabulary, calculated on future value, and requiring complex mathematical and instinctual skill; those practising in this field required little or no capital but extraordinary mental energy. Even those without these natural abilities could afford to dabble in new areas of commerce. Securing finance for their infant 'dot-com' ideas proved relatively easy. Some of these individuals seemed impervious to concern over their levels of debt. As forecast by the astro-economists, it would be some of these individuals who would experience the planetary drama of May 2000 at first hand.

Fears were realised. In April 2000, Jupiter and Saturn began to close in on one another, both forming right-angles with Uranus and Neptune. Back on Earth, pressure was growing for the new industries to show tangible returns. A fall in market values was deemed inevitable. Meanwhile, the faster-moving planets, like wards in the mechanism of a lock, were aligning with the Jupiter–Saturn combination. With tension above mirrored by tension below, a catastrophe of one sort or another was ready to take place.

The astro-economists had made one other major forecast for this period. Using their understanding of the symbolism associated with each of the planets, and having analysed previous events of a similar nature, they feared that a computer virus might be unleashed. They further suspected that this would have dire consequences for the global banking community. As if on cue, the so-called 'love bug' created widespread chaos in the early hours of May 2,[8] just as the planet formation held most tension. It was symbolic of the potential for weaknesses in technical networks that was to be exposed under this configuration. That the banking industry was not more affected was a minor miracle during a month of technological dis-ease.

Many investors were stunned by the fall in stock value of companies whose names they had come to trust. Others felt that the market would recover. Those adding analysis of planetary motion to their decision-making were not as confident. Forecasts of total market meltdown may not have been realised, but the outlook still looked grim for those keeping a weather eye on cosmic activity and planet positions.

Our entire solar system is revolving around a point known as the Galactic Centre.[9] Although this point is also moving, as our local galaxy revolves around yet another point in a spiral of cosmic activity, the position changes very little: around one degree every hundred years.[10] Astro-historians have discovered a correlation between movements of the planets across this particular degree (even though the planets themselves are light years away from it), and particular types of activity. For the last hundred years, as Saturn has moved across this point or has been at 180 degrees from it, global markets have fallen. The astro-economists, aware that Saturn would not pass this degree until the early part of 2003, felt that global markets could not recover until at least that time.

Before then, Jupiter would also travel to a position opposite the Galactic Centre. If economic history were to repeat itself here too, this would bring about a period of gain. How best, then, could the astro-economic advisor put forward the case for a prolonged period of difficulty? The Jupiter effect would be around just long enough to seduce some investors back into the marketplace, where they could easily be ravaged once more. Even forecasting volatility could not put off some people from re-entering the marketplace. Volatility can bring huge profits and some felt able to surf the waves. Others, though, came to thank their astro-advisors for advice that kept them out of certain industry sectors.

Jupiter, the faster moving of the slower planets involved, moved on quickly and by late summer had crossed into the sign of Gemini – a sign associated with information and communications and, therefore, with the telecommunications industry. As anticipated, Jupiter fulfilled its usual reputation. As it moved through the sign of Gemini (the sign associated with conversation), there was an explosion in the number of people buying mobile phones. Sales rose and the value of certain stocks soared in concert, causing most stock market indices to rise too.

Applying the Brakes |

Astro-economists urged caution. They knew that Saturn, moving at a slower pace, was approaching the sign of Gemini and that its reputation for slamming on the commercial brakes might also be realised. They felt that as soon as Saturn, travelling more slowly than Jupiter, arrived in the sign of Gemini, harsh reality would kick in. This group of analysts felt that a depression in dot-com values would be high-profile throughout the telecommunications sector – and even amongst leading names within it.

To the exact day when Saturn entered the sign of Gemini, the global giant Ericsson announced redundancies[11] and most telecommunications stocks lost value. At the time this seemed incredible. Jupiter, moving just slightly ahead of Saturn, had enhanced the feel-good factor and there was considerable confidence in growth throughout this sector. It was a shock to learn that some of the long-established telecommunications companies could be so vulnerable.

Management would, of course, have been aware of the need to take this action some weeks, if not months, before. Again, the astro-economists, noting that from the heliocentric (sun-centred) view Saturn would reach the sign of Gemini in January 2001,[12] suggested to investors that from the beginning of the year they should keep alert for signs that all was not as well as might be implied. The difference between heliocentric and geocentric timings is usually the time it takes for writing on the wall to move from invisible to visible ink.

If further proof were needed that equities could take some considerable time to recover, it came from knowledge of one other cycle: Saturn and Pluto enjoy a synodic period of approximately 33 years.[13] These two planets would reach the half-way point in their present cycle in 2001. This part of the cycle may be referred to as the Full Moon phase. It is a time of extremes – a time of all or nothing. Again, as viewed from Earth, rather than from the Sun, Saturn and Pluto would hold this relationship to one another for some months – from late summer 2001 to early summer 2002.[14]

Analysis of previous Saturn–Pluto cycles showed that this phase is marked by a period of dramatic scaling down or pruning. In this case, Saturn was slowly moving through Gemini, potentially bringing depression to telecommunications stocks, whilst Pluto was moving through Sagittarius, the opposite sign of the zodiac. Industries associated with the latter sign include long-distance travel, air transport, higher education, publishing, law and religion.

There had been moments in the past when Pluto's presence in a particular zodiac zone had given a hint of the industrial saboteur or terrorist at work. It crossed the mind of more than one forecaster that the opposition of Saturn to Pluto could bring about extreme acts, the impact of which could be particularly negative for any or each of the related industries. Later the destruction on 11 September, of the twin towers (Gemini) affording commercial and banking facilities (Saturn) by terrorist (Pluto) attacks from the air (Sagittarius) was to prove excruciatingly symbolic of the opposition of these two planets.

Only those with extraordinary psychic ability could have foreseen the awful events of that day in September 2001. Yet knowledge of the alignment and positioning of these two planets alone had ensured that astro-economic advice given to both short-term and long-term investors was correct: steer clear of travel-related equities, publishing and even some media stocks through this period.

These advisors were clearly on the right track in identifying May 2000 as just the start of economic woes that would beset global markets and particular industries for a long period. Where they differed from other economic experts was in identifying the particular time-scale involved. It is, perhaps, this ability that sets this group of forecasters apart. Their understanding of planetary positions, coupled with research into human behaviour at previous stages of these cycles, enables them to identify both the types of reaction and the actual time-frame in which they might appear.

Looking Ahead |

Of course, cycles never repeat exactly. From the astrological perspective, each time two planets appear 'in conjunction' (as one in the sky), they start at new places within the tropical zodiac. The interaction with other planet cycles varies too. Each planet duo, when compared with other duos, will be at different phases in their respective journeys around the Sun. It requires the passage of some thousands of years for planet cycles to repeat their solar adventure. But by then, the entire solar system will be moving through a different part of the galaxy itself. Every moment is unique. We may see parallels but never exact repetitions.

Even so, astro-economists are at a distinct advantage when compared with other cycles analysts. Those who work with solar system activity know exactly where and when planets will be aligned. They are able to note the moments when new cycles will begin and can mark important dates in their diaries. Again, thanks to the sterling work of NASA scientists and others, they can project these positions several hundred years into the future – a gift quite unavailable to those working with more regular business cycles.

So what are these astro-economists forecasting for the coming twenty years? Saturn has now opposed the Galactic Centre and investors using planet positions in their decision-making processes are ready to move back into a market that has been depressed and where some prices are seen as low. For some, the time feels right to buy.

Astro-economists are not quite ready to back these moves, however. They know that the Transit of Venus in June 2004[15] – another relatively rare event – when Venus effects an eclipse of the Sun by passing between the Earth and Sun and partially obliterating the light of the latter, could be a cosmic signal for further difficulty in this commercial sector. The fact that this occurs exactly opposite the Galactic Centre is ringing an alarm bell for some astro-forecasters. Venus, the readily acknowledged 'planet of love', is also the planet of hard cash and currency. A crisis occurring at this time could mark the start of another rocky period.

It is well known that global debt is now running at unsustainable levels. A crisis has been waiting in the wings for some time. The arrival of the new

Euro currency may have created further difficulty. The US Dollar has seen a weakening in its position in recent times. It is entirely possible that the Transit of Venus, in June 2004, will see these currencies at logger-heads, resulting in a global currency crisis of catastrophic proportions. As we shall see later in this book, this event alone could prove to be the most important, single incident in the fall of the mighty United States of America into a series of smaller, yet economically significant, units.

Astro-economists have an extraordinary amount of material to work with in assessing changes in human behaviour over the coming years. They are able to assess the probability of particular events occurring and can suggest key indicators that point to inevitability.

In the classic work *Mundane Astrology* by Michael Baigent, Nicholas Campion and Charles Harvey, the collapse of the Soviet Union was forecast. All three world-class planet-cycles analysts were of the opinion that as Pluto reached a particular zodiac degree, disintegration of this union of states was likely. Their forecast was considered either absurd or unrealistic by some commentators – yet was to prove accurate. The intelligence they provided was of considerable benefit to those willing to listen. Alerted to the possibility of this radical political change, some people were prepared for the moment and far from being taken by surprise as events unfolded, were able to position themselves to experience the change at first-hand.

It is now clear that the collapse of the old Soviet Union precipitated an economic earthquake whose aftershocks are still continuing. The authors of *Mundane Astrology* displayed breathtaking astro-historical, astro-political and astro-economic skill in making their forecasts, yet they used very simple techniques to arrive at their conclusion. There can be little doubt that if writing today, they would be considering Pluto's pending transit through an area of the zodiac associated with the formation of the present United States of America. Further, they would be noting another rare alignment on the horizon. The end of the decade promises to be every bit as challenging. Long before 2010, however, events taking place in the world will greatly affect the government of the United States. The disintegration of the Soviet Union took place over a relatively short space of time. The collapse of the United States, whilst as dramatic, may be more prolonged. The early warning signals are apparent now, however, and are likely to coincide with a series of cosmic events.

At the time of the Jupiter–Saturn conjunction in 1981,[16] it seemed unthinkable that the USSR and USA would not be competing as superpowers for decades to come. Before the subsequent conjunction of 2000, however, Russia had emerged as the only super-power of the old Soviet Union; and, far from challenging its old foe, was working with the United States to ensure that weapons of mass destruction did not fall into hands deemed unsuitable. It is quite possible that by the time of the next Jupiter–Saturn conjunction in 2020,[17] the United States of America will be no more, and that another 'Russia' will emerge from the Union of States. The collapse of the USA would clearly have enormous consequences, not least of which would be the emergence of at least one new super-power.

The re-emergence of some of the old Soviet states as acknowledged self-governing nations, the unification of Germany and the expansion of Europe, were considered ill-conceived notions in the early 1980s. Within twenty years these developments had paved the way for new economies to emerge. The demise of the United States of America may appear unthinkable now, but by 2020 it is probable. This event too would change the economic and political landscape beyond present imagination. Yet it could happen. History shows the United States to be as vulnerable to certain alignments as was the old USSR. Even a cursory look over American history in relation to planet cycles suggests that the coming years will see immense change in its position on the world stage. The possibility of the United States of America experiencing major transformation cannot be dismissed.

5 Transformation

The interplay between Neptune and Pluto over the next twenty years suggests that the cycle of booms and busts will continue. Pinpointing the exact moments when these could occur, however, requires analysis of the integration of this cycle with others. The two planets have both moved through the zodiac since their last meeting (conjunction) in 1891. Neptune has now completed two-thirds of an orbit since that year whilst Pluto came to the half-way point a few years ago. Analysis of Pluto's movements through each sector of the zodiac is helpful in identifying where economic fault lines might occur.

Pluto takes just short of a quarter-millennium to travel through all twelve signs of the tropical zodiac. Even if medical breakthroughs allow for humans to live far longer than four score years and ten, it is most unlikely that we could live to the approximately 246 years it would require for Pluto to return to the position held at our birth. So, as it passes through each successive sign, any effect is 'new' to us. Of course, family memorabilia may give us a hint of difficulties faced by earlier generations, and closer scrutiny may allow us to observe that these earlier generations lived through similar squalls to our own times. This may help us better understand the present. The legacy in our genes may offer assistance. Even so, essentially we are sailing through unchartered waters.

Pluto does not spend an equal amount of time passing through each sign, as the orbits of the planets are not perfect circles. Their journey describes an ellipse. As an ellipse, by definition, has two foci, it would be most satisfactory if astro-physicists were one day to discover that our Sun's position is matched by a similar focal point where once a sun had been. As yet, however, it is not known if our Sun was ever part of a binary star system. Perhaps there is a black hole at the centre of our solar system and perhaps, as a planet's orbit takes it closer to this point, a particular effect is felt.

Whatever the cause of this elliptical movement, Pluto, like all the planets, takes longer to travel through certain segments or signs of our defined zodiac than others. Pluto's epic journey of 246 years cannot, then, be divided into twelve equal units. For example, it took just twelve years to move through the sign of Scorpio (1982–1994), that part in its journey being close to the Sun, but took the better part of 17 years to move through Taurus (1872–1889) during the aphelion phase of its journey.

At the time of writing, Pluto is moving through the sign of Sagittarius. In 2008 it will move into Capricorn, remaining in that sector of the zodiac until 2023, when it makes its Aquarius ingress – a sign it last visited in the 18th century (1777–1798). Obviously, then, we have no *personal* conscious memory bank to raid in order to assess how we reacted during an earlier transit (though genealogists with an astrological interest may deduce possible themes in family behaviour). Even so, by studying the general history of the periods when Pluto – or any other planet – last visited a sign, we can deduce a possible effect and anticipate reaction. Knowing how our forefathers reacted offers enlightenment – an essential component if we are to assess our future.

Pluto was discovered in 1930.[1] Subsequent analysis of its orbit over the centuries suggests that Pluto's journey has an impact on our collective unconscious – the human memory bank. Much has been written about the mythological link between the use of the name Pluto for this orbiting object and the God of the Underworld. The link is not as tenuous as it might appear. As this planet travels through the zodiac it permits limited access into the often uncomfortable areas associated with each sign: challenging us, with each new visit, to re-learn and to re-evaluate and, importantly, to face any unpalatable truths in areas of human endeavour associated with that sign.

Pluto has a particular affiliation with the sign of Scorpio. Some analysts have drawn the conclusion that Pluto's visits coincide with periods of regeneration, when all that is weak or wasted is stripped away and when parts showing merit or promise are revitalised. The nature of the sign of Scorpio is such that it has a need to test strength. Commonly, people born under this sign experience tests of their emotional strength. In the corporate world, this manifests as tests of financial strength and ethics. Power struggles are synonymous with both Pluto and the sign of Scorpio.

Pluto's most recent journey through this sign was thrilling, exhausting, demanding and, for some, devastating. Cut-throat deals taking place between 1981 and 1995 saw some corporations swallowing smaller businesses whole. Certain corporations saw an enlargement of their presence in the world. For the moment we will ignore the fact that Neptune's broadly simultaneous traversing of Capricorn ensured that this growth would coincide with growing levels of corruption – more on that later. Hindsight suggests that an apparently unstoppable force allowed mighty empires to be created. Corporate global authority gained extraordinary levels of power and influence. Some might describe this as a time where rampant greed took hold. The financial world changed irrevocably during this period. Indeed, the very nature of commerce and of funding projects moved into a new phase. This was a period of 'survival of the fittest' in corporate terms and there appeared to be little room for ethics and morals – attributes that fall more closely under the domain of Sagittarius, the next sign along.

Pluto reached Sagittarius in the mid-1990s, bringing with it a collective need to face ethical issues and to question morality. Indeed, the first years of the new millennium are now yielding uncomfortable truths as to the nature of business itself. Some businesses are already coming unstuck as regards the manipulation of truth and the inaccuracy of their audit reporting – nor are they the only institutions facing awkward questions.

Those born under the sign of Sagittarius share a common quest to expand their horizons – usually through experiencing life in different cultural situations. A thirst for learning requires that the active mind is kept busy by asking questions of a philosophical nature. In keeping with Pluto's ability to unearth that which is hidden, some unpalatable truths concerning the immorality of certain individuals – even those who 'wear the cloth' – have to be faced as Pluto moves through this sector of the zodiac. A religious mantle provides no escape from the truth-seekers. The Catholic Church is unlikely to be the only religious institution facing difficulties as Pluto travels through this sign. As it faces a legal hullabaloo it may find, along with the corporate entities mentioned above, that the penalties for misbehaviour in the past will rock its very foundations.

Sagittarius is also the sign associated with knowledge – not simple knowledge as in basic numeracy and literacy, but a more complex learning that questions the need for the information itself and the quality of the information that is provided. Universities – institutions dedicated to knowledge and truth – will feel the effects of Pluto's voyage through Sagittarius. Teaching and funding will come under scrutiny, with endless debate as to how these places, dedicated to advancing the scope of human knowledge, can aspire to the purest of thought while being dependent on funds from commercial bodies – or even governments with a vested interest in the outcome of studies. Where once 'the body of scientific evidence' stood for detached, scrupulous forensic evidence, the phrase may attract the derision that 'creative accounting' has acquired. Those who were once proud of their affiliation to a particular university or research centre may one day come to rue their involvement.

As we know, there are any number of commercial enterprises in the world today. Some have a clearly defined affiliation with one sign of the zodiac or another. Sagittarius, the half-man, half-horse, is the sign of the traveller. Sagittarius people may enjoy great mental journeys. Some might even be classed as eternal students. Journeys of the mind (via higher education) are just one expression of this sign at work. In business, enterprises associated with this sign include those connected to the travel industry – specifically those related to long-distance travel. The air and shipping industries that cover vast areas of the world come under the broad umbrella of Sagittarius-ruled ventures. Pluto's passage through this sign has been particularly worrying. Here the God of the Underworld, in his disguise as international terrorist, has devalued many global travel networks, bringing some airlines to the brink of bankruptcy and pushing others into a commercial abyss.

The telecommunications industry, too, comes under the broad umbrella of this sign now that global communications have become commonplace. These businesses have suffered incalculably since Pluto, the master of deconstruction before reconstruction, made its way through this sign. In the opening years of Pluto's trip through Sagittarius, licences were sold by the government for hugely inflated figures only to be shown within just a short time to be wildly overvalued.

Pluto can create mayhem most obviously in the businesses or enterprises associated with the sign through which it is passing. Less than a decade ago, few would have imagined that priests would be facing charges of sexual assault, or that Enron, WorldCom and others would be brought down as a result of dishonest accounting, or that global terrorism would bring an entire industry to its knees.

Of course, the history of these happenings began long before Pluto reached Sagittarius. With Pluto firmly established in its passage through the sign, however, seamy underworlds were exposed. Investors may regret entrusting capital to the telecommunications industries, the dot-coms and even airlines. By contrast, others, notably those investing in protection services, anti-terrorist devices and security systems, may see their investments grow fast and furiously in the coming few years. A cursory knowledge of the potential effect of Pluto's passage through any sign gives a clear indication as to which types of industries will go through intensive re-evaluation. Equally, it is possible to see which industries might thrive in the slip-stream.

Fragile Sectors from 2008 |

Those who were aware that Pluto's Sagittarius transit was likely to affect (severely) the travel industry had ample time to reduce their holdings in this sector. Having benefited from this information, this same group is showing a determination to know which industries might be affected by Pluto's Capricorn odyssey (2008–2023).

Capricorn is the sign associated with all that is established – most notably government, and government agencies. Yet it also covers business institutions that have apparently stood the test of time: those firms and corporate names that earlier generations would have found familiar – including household names that have become synonymous with their products. Perhaps the most recognisable of these are the banks and building societies.

The banks of different nations are often seen as citadels. During Pluto's sojourn through Capricorn, their reformation is likely. There were few national banks around during Pluto's earlier visit to this sign (1762–78), but it can be shown that Pluto's Capricorn transit changed the way even these early institutions worked during the period. Many of today's banks will be experiencing this transit for the first time and, as they have no prior experience of the effect, they could react wildly. As we have seen with the travel industry, the effect of a Pluto transit is often to destroy almost totally before re-forming. The banking cupboards may be found to be bare, or have insufficient funds to remain solvent throughout the coming period. Indeed, the very wealth of nations could be compromised. The World Bank itself may be shown to be corrupt, inefficient or both.

Banking systems generally will probably suffer greatly as lack of investor confidence combines with mass withdrawal of funds. With interest rates likely to stay low, many people may feel that their cash is safer under the mattress than in the hands of these bodies. Until now, government bonds have been seen as a relatively safe haven. In the face of extraordinary pressure during this period even these bonds are likely to be found wanting. Governments previously thought of as safe and reliable are likely to default on payments in the coming decade. In part this is understandable: global debt now runs into trillions of dollars and it may be that by the time Pluto reaches Capricorn, this particular bubble too will be ready to burst. Indeed, before 2020 a crisis of faith in the global banking system could give way to alternative systems of money transfer altogether.

It is quite possible that general savings funds will be insufficient to sustain long-term needs. The threatened pension crisis that is hitting headlines looks likely to become a reality. There may be no alternative other than to continue working after the age of 65. Many may welcome this. Others, however, and particularly those whose health is less robust, could find pressure to continue working for a further few years both stressful and unfair. Legislating for retirement age to be lifted from 65 to 75 is likely to encounter fierce resistance by some – though most definitely not by all.

There is a strong link between the sign of Capricorn, its ruling planet, Saturn, and property matters. Those born under this sign would seem to be driven by a need to provide adequately for themselves and their families. If they own businesses, they are very often handed down from parent to child. The most basic concept of putting a roof over the family heads is high on the Capricorn priority list. They expect to work for this too. Saturn takes just under thirty years to make its journey around the zodiac and this has, roughly, been the period of many mortgages. Investment in property has been a feature of financial life for recent generations. Many have seen the value of their homes escalate during the period of the mortgage and so have been able to shorten the mortgage term or assist a younger generation in their first steps onto the property ladder.

It has been assumed by many that a house is an asset and that its value will grow. This situation is likely to change dramatically in the coming years. Those changes are already beginning. First the term of a mortgage has grown. Not infrequently people have borrowed up to three times their joint income, to be paid back not within a Saturn cycle but within an extended (35-year) term. Mention has even been made of introducing the 100-year mortgage, as available in Japan. In such a situation, the debt is carried from one generation to another. The falling stock markets of the early 2000s have already led to forecasts of shortfalls on both endowment and pension mortgages. Possible 'solutions' to this serious situation have yet to be aired. Extending the terms of a debt and demanding that it be met by future generations could be considered an option in the coming years.

Yet another possibility is that the housing market will collapse. In the United Kingdom, it has been felt that 'the Englishman's home is his castle'. It will be interesting to see if this statement still holds true by the time Pluto makes its way through Capricorn (2008–2023). 'Collapsing castles' is not beyond the scope of the imagination for this period. Nor need this effect be limited to the UK. The United States, Canada and Australia are likely to experience turbulence in their housing markets also. In part, this could be fundamental. The expected change in weather patterns could create unsafe conditions in some areas. Older properties are likely to experience severe pressures, making fresh under-pinning of their foundations essential. This trend alone would devalue properties.

There is a clear resonance between Pluto's transits through the signs and changes in taxation. During Pluto's Scorpio journey the focus was on taxation of companies; in the UK through increased Capital Gains Tax and Corporation taxes. During Pluto's journey through Sagittarius new air-traffic taxes were put in place. As Pluto moves on into Capricorn (2008–2023), it seems likely that issues around tax and inheritance will come to the surface. It is also probable that governments will find tax revenue to be substantially different from their forecasts. Clearly, this would have an impact on the provision of essential services.

With other factors suggesting that global warfare could be a feature of 2008–2011, governments may find it prudent to move administration centres yet further away from capital cities. Focused effort to collect taxes might also lead to an expansion in the number of tax collectors. Stealth taxation is likely to escalate from 2008 with even the most basic of services and goods incurring tax penalties.

Waste management, too, comes under the spotlight as Pluto enters Capricorn. Not only will corporate bodies find themselves accountable for clearing-up operations but people themselves may be charged according to the weight and types of waste they create. Whole areas of waste management are likely to be affected by this transit. In the UK, Victorian sewer systems may collapse or warrant vast investment. In other areas of the world, the need to provide basic waste-management systems will take on new urgency.

Water is also likely to hit the headlines once Pluto arrives in Capricorn. Its basic properties come under scrutiny. It is already known that water exists even in the heart of the Sun. It is an extraordinary substance. It is also vital to life. The possibility of corrupted water supplies coupled with the knowledge that certain types of water – that from deep and hidden wells – has a dramatic effect on life on Earth, places water at the centre of power struggles. We should expect the cost of clean and pure water to increase dramatically and for shares in water companies to rise. Water purification companies and related industries are also set to thrive.

In 2001, the travel industry was brought to its knees by an act of terrorism. Disagreements between nations, and the breakdown of international trade agreements, threaten the future of global corporations after 2008. It is hard to see how some major corporations will survive. Extraordinary down-sizing is likely to take place as those companies which swallowed smaller outfits in the 1980s and 1990s find that they can no longer maintain service in a new world climate. The break-up of large corporations may be a particular feature of the coming decade.

This has clear implications for investors. If the old 'blue-chip' companies find themselves unable to operate to the same degree, their dividends are likely to be cut. Just as banks are unlikely to be able to offer secure returns, funds focusing on older, previously reliable businesses that are now showing signs of strain, may find themselves in serious difficulty.

As always, when one sector suffers, another rises to dominance. Although the travel industry suffered appallingly in the early 2000s, those providing security systems fared rather better. Whether this was as a direct service (security guard patrols, secure baggage handling, ticket database management or or through provision of products such as mini-padlocks for luggage), growth was possible for those alert and able to respond to the need.

With attitudes to care and responsibility coming under particular scrutiny as Pluto makes its way through Capricorn, the role of the family may be tested. In the early stages of this transit, perhaps through to approximately 2013, considerable pressure may be put on the family to look after its own – investing in the education of the young and the long-term care of its elderly. Families may be encouraged to live together; incentives made available to enable them to do so. The housing market will be affected. It is probable that we will see a return to the larger houses of old. Flats may be converted back into family homes – with government grants made available to those undertaking this type of work.

The latter stage of Pluto's Capricorn journey carries with it a different impetus. From 2013 to 2023, there could be a growing trend away from the traditional family that features during the early stage of the transit.

Driven by the number of people seeking ways to show that they are a 'family' – though perhaps not connected by genes – the government of the day may have to concede family-type status to groups of individuals choosing to live together and happy to accept long-term responsibility for one another.

Correlations between Pluto's passage through Capricorn and changes in family, political and corporate structures appear formidable. The effect on government is likely to be shattering. Erosion of confidence is probable. Whereas during Pluto's passage through Sagittarius the need has been to find politicians of sufficient moral fibre to hold office, the new quest is likely to be to find people of authority who can ensure that public services continue to be available as required. Difficulties in maintaining tax revenue in a world of tax havens and virtual shopping could make the task hard indeed.

It is, of course, possible to identify the dates when some countries came into being. Indeed, there are some nations whose citizens so identify with their national birthday that they celebrate the date year on year. In effect, they are celebrating the position of the stars and planets at a given period. This cosmic imprint appears to have remarkable import, and as the planets move overhead and make contact with those original positions, national characteristics – latent or commonly observed – come to the surface.

Since it is possible to predict exactly where Pluto (or any other planet) will be at any given date, it is therefore possible to forecast when a nation or country might undergo the type of profound change that is synonymous with this planet at work. All nations will be affected to a greater or lesser degree by Pluto's journey through Capricorn but the one nation that is likely to dominate the headlines through this period could be the United States of America.

6 Collapse of the USA

The land we recognise as the United States of America existed millions of years prior to the date in 1776 when the Declaration of Independence was signed. However, it is on 4 July,[1] during the period when the Sun is making its passage through the sign of Cancer, that the peoples of this vast tract of land celebrate with an annual national birthday party that eclipses other anniversaries. In celebrating this event, Americans choose to put aside the fact that the states were incorporated into the Union at different times. Undoubtedly they view commemoration of the declaration as having an important meaning which benefits from annual reinforcement. The condition of the cosmos and alignment of the planets of the solar system on that day may not be uppermost in the minds of American citizens, yet they are tuning in to the resonances of a momentous day in their collective history.

It seems inconceivable now that there might ever be a time when these celebrations would not take place. Yet, by 2020, these festivities may be changed beyond recognition, and in some states could be supplanted by celebrations of different dates – even if some cling to a much-loved tradition.

America is one of the Cancer nations of the world,[2] i.e. it celebrates its 'birthday' during a period of the year when the Sun is passing through the tropical sign of Cancer. If each sign may be said to have a quest, the Cancer quest is to care, nurture and protect. In America's case, this is exemplified in Emma Lazarus's poem 'The New Colossus', written of the Statue of Liberty at America's 'front door':

> "Give me your tired, your poor,
> Your huddled masses yearning to breathe free,

The wretched refuse of your teeming shore.
Send these, the homeless, tempest-tost to me,
I lift my lamp beside the golden door!"

The American birth-date differs by 75 years, and so has a very different cosmological identity from that of its northern neighbour, Canada. The Declaration of Independence was signed within days of the Sun's conjunction with Jupiter in the sign of Cancer – a very different configuration from when Canada came into being – and an alignment which can only take place in one out of twelve years when Jupiter is making its passage through that sign.

Jupiter is colossal. It is larger than all the other planets put together and spins on its axis faster than the other known planets.[3] It is a 'planet of excess' and arguably the 'super-planet' of the known solar system. During the course of any year, there will be at least one day when, as viewed from Earth, it will appear to be in line (conjunct) with the Sun. Such days tend to be outstanding. With the Sun and Jupiter close together in the chart for the Declaration of American Independence, America stands out amongst the ranks of other 'Cancer' countries. The solar quest is amplified: it becomes 'super-America', outranking Canada and other Cancer nations who did not evolve on one of these special dates in the year. Further, as might be expected, it is not silent about these ambitions; it ensures that everyone is clear about its goals. The very fact that the aims and objectives of this huge nation are emblazoned on a statue situated at its front door, is symbolic of its desire to ensure that everyone is aware of its intentions. Others may harbour similar aims, yet none feel the need to be as public in their quest.

This feature of America's cosmic signature implies grandeur. With the two brightest lights in the solar system (excluding the Moon) coming together, this cosmic signature radiates superiority. Like Icarus, however, it is possible that America may fly too close to the face of the Sun and that within the next twenty years, it will experience hubris.

It may be that the movements of the smallest of the solar system's planets coincide with, at the very least, a period of disarray and internal tension for this great nation. Positioned at the known edge of the solar system, Pluto takes nearly a quarter of a millennium to travel through all the signs of the zodiac. Humans cannot live long enough to experience it in every area of the sky, but nations can. America will experience its first Pluto 'return' (i.e. Pluto will return to the position it held on 4 July 1776) before 2020. This anniversary is likely to prove momentous and may well coincide with the disintegration of the Union.

As noted, the fifty states that make up the Union did not all sign allegiance to one another in 1776 and it is interesting to note the dates and periods when each was incorporated under the Stars and Stripes flag. With each state's signature, the Union has grown and strengthened. The whole benefits from the resources brought under its umbrella. Pluto's role in the empowering of the United States and its subsequent status as a super-power is not to be under-estimated. However, an alignment of this planet with the cosmic formations of 1776 might very well signal its disintegration.

Of course it is entirely possible that Pluto's return to the position it held in July 1776 will pass unnoticed. Forecasting the opposite is based on knowledge of the correlation between Pluto's passage through the zodiac over the last two hundred years and the contacts it has made with the positions held by all the planets in 1776. Here, even the most cursory study yields surprising results. Twentieth-century American history is replete with examples of coincidences between exact planet alignments and events.

It is undeniable that America is empowered through its corporate bodies and that, from the moment of the Declaration of Independence, it was recognised that power, growth and regeneration would come about through the building and nurture of enterprise. The Declaration of Independence demanded that every American citizen have the implicit right to build his or her own empire.

In 1912, Pluto began a 27-year journey through the sign of Cancer[4] – America's 'sun-sign'. During the first half of this transit (until the mid-1920s), as Pluto made its way across the degrees held on that fateful day in 1776 by both the Sun and Jupiter, America became a powerhouse for all kinds of enterprise. Its stature on the world stage grew as it absorbed an extraordinary number of refugees, many of whom rapidly embraced the growing culture of opportunity. America, the apparent 'land of plenty', made good use of the talents of its growing citizenship. Skills that had been devalued or rejected elsewhere, were nurtured and found precious within America's shores. America drew on these resources and gained through the talents of an eclectic population. Setbacks rapidly became opportunities for different groups of people. There was room for everyone and anyone to take advantage of the entrepreneurial culture. In time, the stock market boomed.

Cracks began to appear as Pluto took up traditionally negative aspects to the positions the planets had held at that earlier time. Painful lessons were learned when the stock market crashed in October 1929.[5] As we know, this was followed by a long period of gloom. America struggled and fell into economic depression. Recovery from those dark days was difficult. Yet the American entrepreneurial spirit could not be crushed, and by the time Pluto had travelled a half-orbit, regeneration was firmly underway. Meanwhile, a continuing flow of refugees from Europe brought new resources to a country in desperate need of new blood. The difficulties faced by these displaced people were enormous. Yet together with the settled inhabitants of this huge country, they were able to make progress and to enable the American economy to recover.

On a different stage, Pluto was empowering the nation in a different way. American scientists pushed forward the barriers of physics with the splitting of the atom. With this event, the nation's future military capabilities were to be changed forever, whilst its super-power status was assured.

Pluto's sojourn through Cancer and its eventual positioning opposite its post at the birth of the nation place proved a traumatic period. America emerged from this period both embattled and enriched. Indeed, when just a short time later it experienced the unexpected and devastating attack on its naval base at Pearl Harbor, the Japanese Commander Yamomoto is credited with the saying that the Japanese nation had woken a sleeping giant.[6] America was changed forever by this act of aggression. Great effort was spent to further improve her security.

If Pluto's journey through Cancer was traumatic for the American people, there is every reason to suppose that the planet's return to its position at the birth of the nation will be similarly challenging and exhausting for the nation. In 1776, Pluto was positioned in the tropical zodiac sign of Capricorn; Pluto enters this sign again in 2008. During the planet's journey through this sign it will oppose the Sun and Jupiter positions of 1776. As we saw earlier, it is the Sun's close proximity to Jupiter in the nation's chart that marks it out amongst other 'Cancer' nations. It would be entirely in keeping for America's position in the world to be undermined at the end of the decade if Pluto makes its mark. Internal strife is as likely as tension between the US and other nations. The cohesion of the nation will be compromised through this period. When other important factors are taken into consideration, stress could prove intolerable and, for a time at least, tear at the nation's heart.

As shown earlier, it took 26 years (1912–1937) for Pluto to pass through the sign of Cancer. It will take a slightly shorter period to pass through the sign of Capricorn (2008–2023). Within this time-frame, the years 2010 to 2018 offer a roller-coaster ride that may prove every bit as challenging as 1927 to 1935. There will be little time to absorb the impact of one challenge before the next is on the horizon. Serious cracks in the fabric of American society are likely to show from 2008, culminating in the need for soul-searching and total reappraisal by 2013.

The key years are 2010 and 2011, when Pluto will oppose the positions held by the Sun and Jupiter in 1776. This will be the first time that this planet pattern has occurred since the Declaration of Independence. It is likely to prove an exceptionally difficult period for the American administration. Further, it could be that the United States of America as we know it in the opening years of the 21st century, will lose supremacy and return – if only temporarily – to a fractured land of individual states. The administration will no doubt find maintaining the Union demands as much attention as protecting the whole from international attack.

During 2010 and 2011 the planets will move into a formidable configuration. This, of course, will affect *all* nations, many of whom could find themselves at odds with neighbours. The fact that the alignment homes in on important zodiac degree areas for the United States, suggests that this great nation may be a key player on the international stage through these years. In this the nation may not have the full co-operation of all of her citizens, however. This issue could cause an internal struggle that strikes at the country's heart. Indeed, the process of setting the stage for this event may be underway even now. Many citizens of the United States have declared unhappiness with American involvement in Iraq and Afghanistan. These individuals, many of whom may be relatively recent immigrants to the US, could express considerable disquiet at further involvement in hostilities many miles from their own shores and which might involve American forces taking action in areas of the world which they once considered to be home.

Presidential Inaugurations

The American Constitution defines a specific date for the inauguration of the President and allows a period for the hand-over of administration. In the early part of the 20th century (until 1934) this date was March 4[7] – when the Sun was moving through the tropical sign of Pisces. Each of these Presidencies was driven by the Pisces quest, which is to do something for everyone – whatever their abilities or history. This blended well with the national chart, whose Sun lies in Cancer. Both Cancer and Pisces come from the Water group of signs. The inaugural addresses made by Presidents who began their terms of office under the sign of Pisces are notable for the way in which every citizen was intended to feel a part of the American dream.

In bringing the inauguration forward by some weeks, that emphasis was changed. With the exceptions of President Truman who took the Oath of Office on 12 April 1945, and Gerald Ford, who took the Oath of Office on 9 August 1974,[8] inaugurations since 1934 have taken place on 20 January[9] (or 21 January when the 20th falls on a Sunday), when the Sun is just moving into the sign of Aquarius.

A central part of the Aquarius quest is to find new and innovative ways in which to approach the future. Few would quarrel with the fact that America has been at the cutting edge in the last eighty years. She has accepted new technologies and willingly embraced the idea of looking to the stars and beyond. Indeed, Presidents – the leaders of the United States – who have taken their Oath of Office with the Sun in this sign have made much of the desire to embrace a 'better future' for all.

Comparison between the various inauguration speeches and actual moments of Oaths of Office gives insights into the nature of each of the various Presidencies: the 'Camelot' style of the Presidency of John F. Kennedy encapsulated – by strong contacts to Saturn and Neptune at the moment of taking the Oath – the desire to make a dream reality. Other Presidents' speeches have suggested rather different styles and ethics.

The first US President of the 21st century, George W. Bush (date of birth 6 July 1946[10] – born under the sign of Cancer), swore his oath at noon on 20 January 2001.[11] With both nation and President sharing the same tropical zodiac sun-sign, Cancer, issues concerned with protection and security were always likely to move to the top of the agenda. Other cosmic coincidences were at work on this date (indeed it was analysis of this information that enabled the forecast that Bush would win over Gore). Neptune was conjunct with the Sun that day. Neptune's journey around the Sun takes approximately 146[12] years and it is certainly not true that there has been a Sun–Neptune aspect apparent on the day of every inauguration. The importance of this configuration cannot be over-stated. There is considerable evidence to show that this first presidency of the 21st century will be very different from previous presidencies – it is even possible that it may be the last of its kind.

The Neptune factor was at work in the weeks before the event itself.

Confusion (a Neptune word) around the election results ensured that this presidency was greeted with a variety of emotions. Some felt the post to have been illegally obtained, others felt it to be the signature of a weak presidency, whereas others clearly saw the transfer of authority from Democrat to Republican as offering fresh possibilities – most particularly those representing corporate America.

Neptune is the planet associated with all that seems boundless or even intangible. It 'rules' the sea and is similarly associated with oil. It is also associated with the movie industry, glamour and the fine arts. It is often part of planetary configurations in place where creative accountancy has been at work. Fraud and deception can be as much in evidence as spin and the doctoring of facts. It is entirely in keeping with the nature of the planetary configuration that marked the start of the George W. Bush presidency, for it to coincide with the bursting of a corporate bubble. The collapse of both Enron and WorldCom could be viewed as part and parcel of the themes playing in the sky through this period. It was clear from the start of this presidency that the new CEO of corporate America was facing an array of economic difficulties.

The inauguration of the President of the United States of America is one of the most public events in the world, broadcast across the globe. The President has the attention of the wider international community as well as the citizens of his country as the agenda for the coming four years is set out. The importance of the first speech made by the incoming President cannot be over-stated. Statements made therein let the rest of the world know how this great super-state intends to conduct its affairs for the term of the presidency. Clues may then be drawn as to how trade and international relations may be conducted with the new administration.

The Earth turns on its twenty-four-hour axis so that each degree of the zodiac rises and falls, taking an average of four minutes to do so. As with previous Presidents, George W. Bush took the presidential oath a little after noon. At this time on 20 January 2001, the planet Mars was setting on the horizon. This cannot happen at the inauguration of every President. To 'catch the moment' at which Mars, the God of War, was in this position is remarkable, and immediately drew attention to the possibility of a war-like presidency and, indeed, of attacks upon the presidency itself. Within a few weeks of George W. Bush taking office, someone attacked the White House. Still to come were the appalling events of 11 September 2001, which thrust a stunned nation into an entirely new era with the fight against terrorism at its heart. History may show that the aggressive nature of this

50

presidency contributed to an explosion of anger against the American peoples later in the decade. Recent events in Iraq do little to dispel this possibility.

Astro-geographic techniques used in conjunction with the horoscope of any leader give clues as to where that leader would feel motivated to take part in military struggle (Margaret Thatcher's 'war lines' lie close to the Falkland Islands[13]). Not every national leader goes to war, of course, but for those who begin their term of office under war-like aspects, such personal 'war' areas should be studied closely as potential war zones.

As might be expected given the events of 2001, the astro-geography of the moment of George W. Bush's inauguration showed 'war lines' through part of Afghanistan and an area down through Iraq. George W.'s personal astro-geography – just like his father's[14] – pinpointed an area close to Baghdad itself. It is probable that this region of the world will have a key role to play throughout this presidency – and perhaps beyond. The fact that two presidents share 'war' lines through this area is of concern. The legacy of one war is left for the other. Prolonged military involvement in this area could have repercussions for the end of the decade too – though it will be necessary to assess the astro-geography of those presidents taking office after George W. Bush before the full impact can be estimated. Developments thus far are worrying, however, and the long-term presence of American troops in the region could be a factor in subsequent and even more devastating disputes.

With the position of the planets known well in advance of any period, it was recognised that the incumbent of the Oval Office in the early years of the new millennium would have to steer the country through a difficult period. Not only would this president have to negotiate the Saturn–Pluto opposition of 2001 and the likely economic problems this would bring, he would also have to ride the pressures of Saturn's passage through the USA's own birth-sign of Cancer (June 2003 to June 2005). Saturn's journey through the zodiac is far shorter than that of Pluto, but its impact is still dramatic. The frequency with which it makes contact with certain degrees of the zodiac does little to dispel the impact when it occurs.

Presidential Challenges

During the 20th century, Saturn passed through the sign of Cancer three times: 1914 to 1916, mid-1944 to mid-1946 and late 1973 to 1976. Saturn is a planet with rings – a near perfect symbolism of the responsibilities and constraints that weigh heavily when the planet is prominently placed. As we have seen, America is a Cancer-born nation. It takes pride in protecting its own and declares the aim of ensuring each and every citizen is treated equally. As might be expected, when Saturn passes through Cancer, these aims are challenged. Issues about workers' rights and the protection of citizens dominate.

In 1914, President Woodrow Wilson presented anti-trust legislation[15] to Congress and established a Federal Trade Commission to prohibit unfair business practices. This was followed, towards the end of Saturn's stay in Cancer in 1916, by a new law prohibiting child labour.[16] Workers' rights were also enforced by limiting railroad workers' hours to eight a day.[17] Typically, the need to protect and nurture the vulnerable came to the surface during this period.

Saturn was in Cancer again through the mid-1940s. Both President Roosevelt and President Harry S. Truman experienced the weight of office at this time. Truman became President on 12 April 1945[18] and later told reporters, 'I felt like the moon, the stars, and all the planets had fallen on me'.[19] As with President Wilson, it fell to him to lead the nation as it faced particular economic and social responsibilities. His legacy, in the form of legislation known as 'The Fair Deal', proposed expansion of Social Security, a full-employment programme, a permanent Fair Employment Practices Act, and public housing and slum clearance.[20]

Two other Presidents experienced the effect in the 20th century. Presidents Nixon and Ford occupied the White House during an extraordinarily difficult period for the American people. President Gerald R. Ford took the Oath of Office on 9 August 1974, the day after Nixon resigned and just as Saturn passed the position held by the Sun on 4 July 1776 – exactly. This was extraordinarily significant. Many individuals experience such a Saturn transit as like having a yoke placed around their neck. Ford's description of this moment, to be found in the text of his inaugural speech, was contained in the following words: 'I assume the Presidency under extraordinary circumstances. This is an hour of history that troubles our minds and hurts our hearts.'[21] Ford's task was to revive a depressed economy, deal with chronic energy shortages, and simultaneously hold on to world peace.

It is clear from the 20th century examples alone that wearing the mantle of office while Saturn passes through Cancer is not at all easy. Saturn makes this transit from June 2003, and a year later passes the position held by the

Sun on the day of the Declaration of Independence. History shows this to be problematic for the President of the time. Presidents Nixon and Ford both found this period traumatic. Of course there is no guarantee that there will be an action replay of the challenges that faced them – the total cosmic picture in the summer of 2004 is very different from that of 1974–6. At the very least it should be anticipated that economic tension will be considerable. Trading agreements with other nations come under pressure as America seeks to protect her own – perhaps using similar mechanisms to those used to protect steel-workers in 2003. It is possible, too, that the cost of maintaining armies in several areas across the globe will put further pressure on the American budget, leaving the President with hard economic choices to make.

Certainly, if history is to repeat, then this period will be tough for the President and his administration. It is not, however, the only planet pressure to be faced over this time. Another, more formidable combination takes effect during the summer months of 2004. Pluto will oppose the position held by Mars at the signing of the Declaration of Independence. This particular planetary combination is traditionally associated with war, violence and painful action. The history of the United States shows it to have experienced it this way before.

As we know, Pluto travels slowly. The alignment in 2004 will be the first of its kind since the Declaration of Independence. There have, however, been two occasions when Pluto has lain at right-angles to Mars's position. This occurred first between 1814 and 1816 and again throughout the greater part of 1967 and 1968. In 1814, Washington DC was burned by British troops.[22] Throughout 1967 and 1968, US troops were involved in the Vietnam War. The striking correlation between the Pluto–Mars effect and acts of violence suggests that the American peoples could experience dramatic military confrontation in 2004.

Of course, it is by no means *inevitable* that physical war will be a factor in the difficulties facing America in the summer of 2004. There are other possibilities: Pluto will still be passing through Sagittarius – the sign associated with truth. It is entirely possible that it will be a war of words as opposed to acts of aggression that takes place in June 2004. It may well be that the President will be faced with a legal crisis and a challenge to his authority not dissimilar to that faced by President Nixon. Whether the fight be over truth or inflamed by international argument, the President's position during this time is unenviable. He could come under personal attack, with his personal code of ethics and religious faith coming under intense scrutiny. At the very least, a sense of isolation around the Presidency is probable. Equally, just as occurred in 1974 when Saturn last held this position, the nation could find itself divided if the people are forced to accept that the administration is not as wholesome as they would wish. Indeed, given the planetary configurations, one has to wonder if George W. Bush will finish his term of office.

Saturn's presence in Cancer is likely to affect corporate America adversely too. Recession is probable. Ever-tighter restraints on costs whilst meeting workers' rights puts pressure on Chief Executives. America may not be alone in experiencing vociferous union activity in 2004, but she may not be well placed to cope. Strikes are possible. With farmers experiencing yet further hardships as a result of bad weather, poor crops, animal disease and lack of capital funding, this same period could witness more foreclosures than have been seen for many years.

Elsewhere, a wave of anti-Americanism diminishes the ability of large corporations to achieve good returns. For rather different reasons, echoes of the collapse of the Enron and WorldCom corporations may be heard too. Other corporate scandals could yet emerge. The possibility of one of these scandals falling near the Presidency must be considered. Indeed, of all the possible pressures that could befall the President in the summer of 2004, this would appear the most likely. It would also set the scene for a growing dilemma for the American people: how to find individuals untainted by scandal, with the talent and integrity to steer America through the coming years.

Economic Stress

The next President of the United States of America should take the Oath of Office at noon on 20 January 2005. At that moment, Chiron will be exactly overhead and in opposition to Saturn still moving through Cancer. This does not augur well. The 'audit' planet is at the top, with the 'headmaster' planet at the bottom of the chart. Not only is this President likely to face difficulties with a populace tired of being at war, it is probable that issues of accountability will resonate throughout the period of office. There is little comfort to be gained by looking at the planet formation for the next Presidency in 2009. The chart for this moment is not dissimilar to that when President Nixon took his Oath of Office. The difference this time is that economic distress is all too apparent. Given that this same month could see real distress in global currencies, it is possible that a decision will be taken to defer the presidential appointment.

Even so, issues around corruption will surely dominate until Pluto returns to its 'starting point' in 2013. Whatever the challenges of summer 2004, they should be seen as minor compared with the problems that will beset a later Presidency when Pluto opposes the solar position in 2010. This transit too will be a 'first' in US history but we may look back to the periods when Pluto has lain at right-angles to this position to find clues as to what might be experienced. Perhaps unsurprisingly, this brings us to difficulties with the nation's finances – with the incumbent President being effectively held to ransom by those with personal fortunes able to use their wealth and influence to help restore the situation.

As is well known, Washington may be the centre of American politics but New York is most certainly the centre of the nation's finances. Clearly the two are linked – when one is challenged, so too is the other. Difficulties faced by the President in 2004 could be mirrored in offices of top firms on Wall Street and, indeed, throughout the boardrooms of America's corporations. These pressures, though, will be minor compared with those likely to occur at the end of the decade.

The economic temperature in New York, and on Wall Street particularly, varies considerably from that of Washington and may have something to do with geographic location. Manhattan is surrounded on three sides by water and exposed to the Atlantic Ocean. The people of this small island are acutely sensitive to prevailing winds and tides. Perhaps because of their changeable environment, they have a volatile reaction to market trends. It may be said that precisely because the tides are an integral part of daily life in Manhattan, the lunar phases and the distance between the Earth and Moon have a particular significance. If this is the case, then the years 2007 to 2009 may be particularly interesting.

The sunspot cycle is expected to reach minima around this time. It is during 2007 that the Moon will make an exceptionally close approach to the Earth, resulting in abnormally high neap (spring) tides. With economic output high, but the administration of the period limiting the flexibility of the nation's entrepreneurs, the incumbent of the Oval Office could experience serious difficulties as a volatile stock-market lurches and eventually threatens to destabilise the nation. This is followed by another stressful angle applying in the first few months of 2009. Again, if history is to repeat, a run on the nation's reserves is probable. The US dollar is not immune to difficulties over these months. Devaluation could occur, resulting in even greater difficulties for the administration. In attempting to maintain control through this economic storm, a few individuals holding high office may be tempted to manipulate the markets. Such behaviour would further underpin the need for the new approach to politics that emerges after 2014.

Corporate America, then, may experience something equivalent to a stroke in 2008/9. The behaviour of the administration of this period could later prove to have fallen far short of what would be considered acceptable. By 2014 many citizens may feel that 'something rotten is at work in the great USA'. With the fall from grace of the President, the role of the presidency itself could suffer as a result. It is around this time that some states could choose to break away from the Union entirely.

Another important feature of the cosmic signature of July 1776 is that the Sun was almost opposite Saturn in the sky. Today's astro-economists view this combination as marking tension between Chief Executive Officer (in this case, the President and the Washington administration) and management (i.e. the nation's financial hub, Wall Street). There is evidence in the history of the United States to show that when this part of its cosmic signature is under pressure, singular events occur.

Between 1834 and 1836 Pluto aligned with this Sun/Saturn pattern. Today's astro-economists, working at that time, might have wondered if the President would sabotage his own position by playing power games with the managers of America Inc., or whether events beyond his control would affect the nation's reserves negatively. There would assuredly be consensus amongst these astro-economists that a power-struggle lay ahead and that the finances of the nation could only suffer as a result.

President Jackson's handling of the nation's reserves[23] prior to 1836 was commendable. He had eliminated the national debt – a considerable feat. The volume of trade on the various American stock exchanges was high and a bull market was underway. On 16 December[24] however, the Great Fire of New York broke out. It raged for two days, and left the heart of New York's financial district in ruins. This could hardly have occurred at a worse time for the developing nation. President Jackson, who held a pathological dislike of paper money, attempted to curb speculation, and decreed that land being sold by the government must be bought using specie – actual gold or silver. His executive order or decree, announced on 11 July,[25] effectively put a run on bank reserves and brought about the downfall of some of the smaller banks, whose gold and currency reserves were inadequate for the demands put on them. It is generally agreed that President Jackson, virtually single-handedly, brought the country from boom to bust in the

56

space of less than a year. The depth of the depression of 1837 has never quite been matched.

This particular Pluto effect was operative again between 1924 and 1926. Once again a bull market was in force. The stock market kept rising – as did credit levels. And as before, the period was followed by a stock-market crash and subsequent depression. This time it was not the presidency itself that suffered but the President himself. President Harding died in office.

President Nixon was in office when the most recent of these Pluto effects was in force. Mauled by the Watergate revelations, he was forced to resign. His vice-President was then sworn in as President. Without doubt President Ford then presided over one of the most difficult periods of American economic history.

Whoever holds office in 2014 will come under similar Pluto pressure. The acknowledged need to separate the President from corporate America gains momentum from 2008. By 2014 it is possible that the position of the then President will be made untenable by the forces around him or her. Accusations of corruption and manipulation are likely to fly, with the incumbent of the Oval Office finally forced to resign. Again, if history is to repeat, then a thriving bull market in 2014 will be brought to a halt and subsequently thrown into reverse by the strategies employed by the President of the day.

The Federal Reserve |

Any review of the position of the USA in the coming twenty years must include an appraisal of the role of the Federal Reserve,[26] which came into being just as Pluto reached the sign of Cancer in 1913. In recent times particularly, but generally since the institution came into being, the Chairman of the Federal Reserve has shown himself to have a ferocious grip on the nation's finances. However, as we shall see in more detail in a later chapter, the Fed comes under direct pressure in 2008. Whether it can survive the pressures of that year and the following twelve months is debatable. Disenchantment with the Federal Reserve's ability to husband the nation's resources gathers momentum from 2006. A growing number of citizens may feel repelled by the decisions taken. This groundswell looks likely to gather pace, so that by 2008 the then Chairman may be faced with an angered citizenship.

The importance of the Galactic Centre has already been discussed. Pluto crosses this point in the last few months of 2006. One of the many possible outcomes is that the United Nations will be superseded by a World Forum. The implications for the United States cannot be over-stressed. The American administration will find itself challenged over and over again. Sanctions might even be taken against the US. Decisions made by the Federal Reserve and the impact these have on other nations come under discussion. To preserve its authority, the Federal Reserve may well take actions that are seen as bullying by some nations. Whether or not the Federal Reserve, as we know it, remains an institution, the behaviour of its administration through this period is likely to be seen as reprehensible – both at the time and later, if it survives, in 2014.

Another aspect of American life likely to hit the headlines in the coming years is scrutiny of the role of certain religious authorities. As we know, arrests (of priests accused of child molestation and evangelical preachers who have abused funding), have already been made. It is probable that what has taken place thus far is just the start of a much bigger campaign that gets underway during 2004 and continues until 2007. This could have particular impact on television stations devoted to charitable giving – affecting both well-established and 'good' charities along with others whose motives are questionable. Both the television stations and the charities involved face tough times. Whilst this is very much a domestic issue, the effect it has on other nations may be considerable. Seeds of hostility towards the USA sown as funds dry up, could provide yet another battlefield early in the next decade when poorer nations recall their treatment. These developments are not to be dismissed lightly as their contribution to later events appears to be considerable.

The immediate picture for the United States is clearly not bright. Good news from some quarters is offset by painful news from across the globe where American service personnel are at work. The number of deaths in military campaigns is likely to reach distressing levels in 2004 and 2005. Further, corporate scandals and economic distress will give many citizens cause for concern. Rumblings of disquiet about pension arrangements will become more vociferous. Meanwhile the President's authority would seem likely to be challenged. The interesting point here is that should he be displaced, the inauguration of the second President of the 21st century would have a very different cosmic signature from the norm. As with President Ford, the oath of allegiance could be taken under a different cosmic vibration.

Important as the next presidency will undoubtedly be (this President will be in office as Pluto passes that all-important Galactic Centre point in 2006), it is the holder(s) of this office from 2008 to 2014 that warrant most attention. The USA will go through a period of extraordinary transformation in these years – and will do so against the background of global stress of a type we have not seen for many thousands of years. By the end of this period, in 2014, the citizens of some states may be considering withdrawing from the Union entirely. It is quite possible that both a north–south and an east–west divide will occur – at least temporarily. By 2015, the term 'super-power' could be applied to specific states, rather than to the Union as a whole.

The role of the Internet in this transformation cannot be exaggerated. The potential for this medium to be used by citizens without the funds presently thought necessary to launch campaigns for office, is now being realised. Throughout 2006, an increasing number of citizens could develop political plans in cyber-space. Indeed, it is possible that it will be one of these individuals with a hidden agenda who creates a mayhem of which the USA will have had no prior experience.

The individual(s) involved may well be suffering delusions of grandeur. The establishment, however, is unlikely to have the required forces to shield itself from this attack. Noting that by this time the US government, along with other western governments, could suffer a devastating fall in tax revenue, it is possible that the President could be held to ransom by these agents. This would have massive implications for the nation's wealth and its national debt.

The World Bank

The cumulative debt of nations could result in catastrophe. Solutions to the growing problem are yet to be presented. Ancient Jewish law demanded that a debt be written off after a number of years. In the Jewish system, a neat ebb and flow permitted both speculation and errors of judgment. This containment of indebtedness arguably stopped further woes from befalling those owing large sums, and prevented both them and their families from falling into penury. Other societies have employed very different methods of debt management.

The extended mortgage, where family members work to reduce costs incurred by an earlier generation, is common in Japan. In both the Jewish and Japanese systems, a code of honour is at work. This is not as apparent elsewhere. Indeed, the present cumulative world debt is not underwritten by honour – or anything else. Sustaining present levels cannot be possible. Certainly, analysis of the phases of the planet cycles at work over the coming decade suggests that the credit bubble might explode – with devastating consequences.

Debt, on some level or other, is experienced by many. Kings and queens, princes and princesses, premiers and dictators have all had experience of owing more than they can pay. History is littered with wars in part created by the need to reduce levels of indebtedness. These wars themselves have often simply displaced the debt elsewhere. In 1944 and 1945, sincere efforts were made to try to resolve this difficulty. It may be that the introduction of those ideas and methods exacerbated the problems, however. The systems put in place then do not appear to have been adequately modified in the ensuing years. Analysis of the cycles unfolding since 1944 and 1945 suggests that a crisis is looming.

Towards the end of World War II it became apparent that large swathes of Europe would require financial help to recover from the effects of nearly half a century of instability. In July 1944, 400 delegates from 44 Allied countries met near Bretton Woods,[1] New Hampshire in the USA, where they agreed on the establishment of a fund that would meet these needs. Agreement to establish an International Monetary Fund (IMF) was reached by 31 July,[2] though not signed and formalised until 27 December[3] of that year. The cosmic activity of the time was extraordinary. It seems clear now that those attending this conference made decisions that are now affecting us all. There was no malevolent intent by these individuals. Even so, the legacy of their decisions has had far-reaching effects and in the coming years appears likely to touch even those who have had no direct dealings with the institution. The star activity over Bretton Woods on the morning of 31 July, as the conference closed, is fascinating. The Sun rose with Sirius – the Dog Star. This star is one of the more famous of the myriad encircling the Earth. It has high magnitude and a particular reputation: the Dogan tribes of Africa celebrated their beliefs in its mystical power. It is generally viewed as being of positive influence, suggesting a desire to work for the greater good. Many would have viewed this as a positive omen. Only closer perusal of the cosmic activity would have yielded disquiet.

At the time when the IMF came into being, there was indeed a focus on the need to 'do something' to halt financial misery and to enable growth. There is little doubt that some sort of finance plan was essential. Now, though, whole nations are in debt to the World Bank that came into being after the creation of the International Monetary Fund, and the full political, environmental and social effects of the decisions it has taken have yet to be quantified. The authority of the two organisations has grown. Even so, they may not survive the cosmic pressures of the next twenty years.

In 1944 the yearly-mean number of sunspots per day was just 9.6.[4] In the latter days of July, the number was just above average for the year, but for most of the month there had been little or no activity. The daily numbers of sunspots increased in the following months, yet even in 1945 they were relatively low, at an average of 33.2 (the numbers can reach over 200).[5] July 1944 was special in that it was a period of particularly low sunspot activity. Is it possible that although there was clearly a desire to arrive at a beneficial system for those in need, there was insufficient human creativity at work to carry this through? Is it further possible that a particular mind-set was given voice during this period and that this attitude was oblivious to the extreme financial dangers that lay ahead?

There was a solar eclipse in July 1944. Solar eclipses are not unusual (there are at least two each year), but the fact that the one that took place on 20 July was both preceded a fortnight before by a lunar eclipse *and* followed just a fortnight later by another lunar eclipse, marks the period out. A solar eclipse will usually be accompanied by a lunar eclipse, but one either side of the event raises its status. It has long been recognised that the close relationship between the Sun, Moon and Earth has an effect on the Earth's surface and, quite possibly, on the behaviour of all life forms. It is known that the geomagnetic field is affected by this cosmic activity. Certainly, analysis of eclipse patterns and historical events suggests that often these cosmic happenings correlate with defining moments in social history.[6] Any solar eclipse may be said to mark both an ending and the beginning of a new chapter in social history. In mundane or world astrology, the position of the Moon provides a description of the people of a nation. The two lunar eclipses of this period suggest that whilst there was much discussion about the needs of people generally, their voices were 'eclipsed'.

There is a further peculiarity about this solar eclipse. Looking way past the position of the Sun and Moon at this moment and far, far out into space, we would eventually come upon a black hole. The study of such cosmic bodies and of their positioning is still in its infancy. This particular black hole is fairly well documented, however. Black Hole M-82 is positioned at 28 degrees Cancer.[7] The one authority on this subject, Phillip Sedgwick[8] of the United States, suggests that when this area of the zodiac is highlighted, there is a desire for a 'policy of complete non-interference regarding others'. It may be said that this is hugely at odds with what subsequently occurred. Here the eclipse looks to have played an exceedingly important role – robbing the zodiac area of its power, perhaps.

What seems clear today is that the real needs of those requiring assistance were not heard. Disparity between those who 'had' (the potential lenders) and those who 'had not' (those in desperate need) perhaps paved the way for institutions that did not listen carefully to the voices of either party. It is doubtful that an experienced astrologer would have advocated the launch of a major institution during this period. It is even more alarming that the final documents were signed within two days of another lunar eclipse. These are not optimum moments for new ventures, and indeed, suggest the potential for hidden agendas.

The chart for the July solar eclipse alone suggests that the idea of a central lending fund may have been thrown together in some haste and that more attention to detail would have been wise. It is interesting to learn, given the extraordinary number of planets in the pleasure-seeking sign of

Leo at the time of the Bretton Woods conference, that recreation – in the form of dancing lessons, theatre trips and sports activity – were dominant activities over the few days of the conference.[9] Some might argue that key members of the group used these activities to stimulate the creative parts of their brains and that their work benefited as a result. Perhaps the concept ion and subsequent formation of the International Monetary Fund was a stroke of creative genius. Nevertheless, the fact that so many nations were not part of the decision-making process would seem to have left a legacy of difficulties. This may have something to do with the extraordinary planet picture of that period. The cosmic weather applying at the time of the fund's conception was distinctly unusual. It appears possible that institutions born as a result of the Bretton Woods agreement of July 1944 may be deeply flawed and that their foundations may be wholly inadequate to withstand the storms that lie ahead.

In July 1944, the known planets – together with the eclipse – spanned a 120-degree section of the zodiac, as though in a fan. This focus on just one-third of the zodiac suggests a certain lop-sidedness of thinking. On a very simple level, it is as though the needs of just a third of the world's population warranted special care and attention.

As explained earlier, there are at least two solar eclipses in any year – sometimes as many as five. Obviously then, there is not an eclipse in every sign in every year. There were just two solar eclipses in 1944, with the summer of that year dominated by the solar eclipse in the sign of Cancer. (The conference took place between an important lunar eclipse (6 July) and the solar eclipse of 20 July. These periods between lunar and solar eclipses have often been found to be windows of opportunity – with some more beneficial than others. Other features of this 'window' suggest that it was a strange time indeed.)

Those born under the sign of Cancer are said to be driven by a desire to protect and nurture. An accent on the concept of 'duty of care' would be felt world-wide over several months. Many successful corporations fall under the influence of this sign and many successful Chief Executives have this sign highlighted. The tendency to nurture an embryonic business, to see it grow, to look after employees and to provide due diligence in service usually ensures longevity, if not triumphant success. The July 1944 solar eclipse, then, suggests that husbandry and good house-keeping of all kinds was a dominant tune playing in the sky through this period.

Cancer people grip on tightly to what they know to be safe, tried and tested. Generally they are creatures of habit. Particularly sensitive to the movement of the Earth's only natural satellite, the Moon, those born under this sign suffer great swings in emotion and reaction mirroring the ever-changing appearance of this celestial body. In what must surely be an attempt to experience security and stability, they develop routines and habits that offer safety and reliability. This can be a very successful mode of behaviour. Statistically it can be shown that those born under this sign tend to be good entrepreneurs and managers.

However, these are not, perhaps, the best traits for a bank or fund. Routines can develop into administrative hoops, with only those who are familiar with the rules and regulations succeeding in obtaining assistance. Another negative manifestation of the Cancer spectrum is that unscrupulous people use their knowledge to personal advantage. Corrupt information networks grow, bringing with them the potential for black-mail. The planet music of this period was not wholly Cancer-dominated, however. Analysis of the rest of the planet picture indicates other themes at work.

Mars's position in Virgo throughout July 1944 accented awareness of the need for attention to overall detail. Combined with an encouraging aspect with Saturn, Mars would have brought a recognition that a meticulous approach has advantages in ensuring efficient administration. That said, it might not have been noted that a disadvantage of this placement is that all-encompassing paperwork and general fussiness can slow down procedures, effectively depriving people of aid at moments of calamity.

Apparently in contrast to this effect, another special feature of the July 1945 eclipse was the number of planets transiting the sign of Leo – one of the Fire signs of the zodiac. Traits associated with this sign include an initial tendency to react quickly – but in an unregulated way. Just as with a forest fire, there is no operating thermostat and events can spin out of control. Without considered and careful assessment, errors of judgment can be made.

In an individual, this behaviour usually results in 100 per cent enthusiasm at the start of a project. The enthusiasm rarely lasts, however, and instead is replaced by sheer doggedness and determination. The norm is for projects to take significantly longer to complete than was originally expected. Initial joy and excitement is then displaced by a grudging feeling that one is honour-bound to complete the task – even if it might be better to abandon it as further information becomes available. Pride here often comes before a fall.

With both Mercury (thinking and talking) and Jupiter (big promises and ideas) travelling through the sign of Leo as the inauguration of a fund was discussed, there existed the potential for those involved instinctively to offer more than could reasonably be delivered. A dogged determination to do what was felt to be 'right' would have marred considered, calm and rational thinking. There is little doubt that there was great enthusiasm for the project. The beat of the cosmic drum would have been compelling. The need to take action and to build a system that allowed defeated nations to stand on their economic feet once more would have been seen as imperative. Indeed, the insistence of the cosmic drum that something *should* be done would have been inspiring, if more than a shade melodramatic.

The power of the cosmic tune playing as the conference got underway would have been seductive, with many delegates supporting the idea of a grant-aiding fund and being naturally predisposed to deal with events on a grandiose scale. This thinking paved the way for the fund to become a lender of last resort. The fund would soon gain the status of 'super-bank', with those requiring its assistance first having to explore other avenues before arriving at its door and receiving assistance.

The Galactic Centre, the point in space around which the Milky Way revolves, measured against the tropical zodiac, moves very, very slowly as the galaxy itself gyrates in the universe. It appears to move at rather less than one degree per century and presently may be found nearing the edge of the sign of Sagittarius. This 'Galactic Point' has been shown to be sensitive. When events 'shake the world', this point has often been activated by the presence of a planet aligned with this degree. It must surely be of great interest to note that at the founding of the IMF, Venus, the planet associated with fairness and balance and with finance, was positioned with the Galactic Centre. The implications are obvious – the new fund would have a dramatic effect upon the finances of the world.

The International Monetary Fund formally came into being six months after the Bretton Woods conference and at a time when the Sun was making its annual visit to the sign of Capricorn. Obviously, the planets had moved on in the six months since the Bretton Woods agreement. The faster planets had moved some distance across the zodiac. Even so, a significant portion of the zodiac circle was unoccupied. Whereas the planets were all contained within a third of a circle at the time of the Bretton Woods meeting, the planets were contained within half of the zodiac circle at the inauguration of the IMF – symbolically dividing those who 'had' from those who 'had not'.

Yet another solar eclipse occurred within a few days of its inception.

This eclipse, occurring just six months after the important Bretton Woods eclipse, lay at the other side of the zodiac, far away from the M-82 Black Hole and in the sign of Capricorn. Capricorn is the sign linked with institutions – mainly those controlled by governments – and with 'big' business, i.e. the multinational companies and conglomerates. Like its opposite sign, Cancer, Capricorn falls into the Cardinal group of signs, indicating a desire to 'do'. Those born under the sign of Capricorn display qualities of action, perseverance and a determination to achieve. They are arguably more aware than other signs of the value of leaving lasting legacies. Those of this sign do not wear their hearts on their sleeve, preferring instead to foster a philosophy of prudence, diligence, and building for the future.

In a very simple way, the IMF may be said to do precisely that. It recognises where there is genuine need, it divorces itself from the pressure of emotional baggage, and applies the principle of 'full steam ahead' to its projects once these have been agreed. There can be little doubt that the IMF has been active. In fact, it has been *extremely* active, lending one-third of a trillion US dollars since its inception. It may not be possible to track exactly the movements of this money using the cycles of the planets, but there are clues. These are suggested by comparing the positions of the slow-moving planets as they move through the zodiac with the positions that the known planets held in July 1944 and, particularly, at the inauguration of the IMF in December 1945.

In considering the formation of the planets at the time of the July 1944 solar eclipse (and the Bretton Woods agreement), it is worth noting that Neptune was the last planet of the 'fan' that spanned just a third of the zodiac area. Whilst faster-moving planets would move into the empty sector in the autumn of that year, Neptune's long, slow journey would be likely to render the greatest drama. The effect would not be dissimilar to depressing the sustaining pedal on a piano while playing a chord – that particular sound would be prolonged though its quality would diminish over time. Using this analogy we can conclude that as Neptune hovered over the positions held by each of the planets, another long, sustained chord would be played. In fact, over the years, rarely has there been a break from this quality of planet 'noise'. It might even be said that the world is so used to this frequency of sound that when this 'pedalling' ceases, we will all be taken by surprise.

Astronomical facts show Neptune to be covered in swirling mists of gases and vapours. The astrological effects operating when this planet aligns with positions in any given chart are to distort, confuse, infiltrate, dissolve, pervade and weaken. These effects are sustained through long periods. The senses are heightened for good or ill. Those under the influence of Neptune are commonly hugely idealistic. They seek an altered state of awareness.

Artists under Neptune's influence produce work that is magical, ethereal and illuminating. Accountants and economists, under similar influence, may lose their grip on reality – the creative accountancy and curious economic thinking that this produces having devastating results. The danger for organisations experiencing the effect of Neptune is that they may become involved in projects that have more spin than content. Commonly there is a lack of clarity and a loosening of budgetary restraints. Projects begun under Neptune's vibrations are most likely to exceed their initial budget with potentially devastating consequences.

Throughout 1982 and 1983, Neptune moved across the Galactic point, conjoining the position of Venus in the IMF chart. As might be expected, this was a curious time for the IMF. History may one day show that this period also marked the time when the accelerator was depressed and world debt took on new momentum. It was in late June 1983 that a coalition of environmental groups demanded that the US Congress consider whether the World Bank (and by implication, the IMF) were harming both the environment and the poor with some of their projects.[10] Even at that stage it was recognised that costs, strategies and debt factors could be creating more problems than were being solved. A treasury official of the time remarked that 'there is no project so costly, and so disastrous, that the Bank won't throw hundreds of millions of dollars into it to try to make it better'.[11] The problem here is that that money had to come from somewhere. Debt escalated.

Neptune slowly moved to oppose Saturn in the IMF chart in the 1980s. At this time, a relaxation (typical Neptune effect) of Saturn (rules, regulation and framework) led to a flood of requests for assistance. The words 'No' and 'Neptune' do not go together. The Neptune influence is to appease and to find ways of doing things. It bends or goes underneath boundaries to achieve its ends. Thus many countries were given financial support for projects without first meeting essential criteria.

Neptune has links with the sea and with water. During its lifetime the IMF has granted a large proportion of funds to the building of dams.[12] Experts from a number of fields deemed that the answer to poverty and hunger was irrigation and the efficient use of available water supplies. In many cases this approach has been disastrous, proving as costly to undo as to begin.

In 1990 the IMF and World Bank together sponsored a project to divert water from the River Narmada in India to irrigate the Gujarat region.[13] The building of the Sardar Sarovar dam was welcomed by the Indian government of the day. But there was a problem. The destruction of several villages was an inevitable consequence. The people living in the adjoining land would have to be moved elsewhere. Village elders were called to study the plans. It was not easy to persuade them to move from their ancient homelands. Drowning the graves of ancestors, their homes and their way of life was an awesome prospect.

Seduced (another Neptune word) finally by the promise of better land, cattle and subsidies, they finally agreed to move. It is hard for any of us to comprehend the enormous challenge this represented to these uprooted people. Worse was to follow. Far from being given the land shown to them, the people were given other areas on which to try to recreate their homeland. These proved to be wastelands owned by the government and on which rent would be due. The displaced people had been sold into slavery and destitution. Their own land, passed from generation to generation, was gone, washed away by millions of gallons of diverted water.

It could not be said that this huge sacrifice (another Neptune word) had achieved the aim of relieving poverty elsewhere. There were problems in building this dam. Some fund money ended up in the hands of unscrupulous and corrupt officials. The materials used were of poor quality and the dam did not do its job. The very infrastructure, needed to support the workers on the project, was also open to corruption. Total costs soared. The possibility of the government repaying the loan – or even meeting interest payments – became less and less likely. As is so typical of the effect of Neptune opposing Saturn, ballooning corruption and fraud made realisation of the dream impossible. By the time Neptune had moved from this position, an ancient people had been displaced, vast sums of money had been lost and many people had become disillusioned, exhausted and broken.[14]

The IMF itself did not collapse from this failure. Its aims and objectives were still intact, even if it should have been carrying a level of shame and attempting some form of recompense. That said, plans were soon put in place to ensure that there would be no recurrence of this disaster. However, even as these new regulations were being implemented, further dam projects were being planned, each of which faced similar problems to those of the Sardar Sarovar. In many cases these dams have proved disastrous for the local economy.

The influx of American dollars lent by the IMF has brought with it awesome levels of corruption. Countries have been left owing far more than the original estimate.[15] Further, to meet initial borrowing criteria they have had to make political and social changes that have not always been in their best interests. More and more of these countries are unable to repay their loans. Their original fragile economies have been fractured by the ideas of people who have little understanding of other countries' national characteristics and ethos. Unless the rules are changed, the peoples of these nations will be in debt for many years to come. Their impoverishment can only grow. There is no way out of their slavery to the ideology presented by the IMF.

It is hard to see how IMF policy can change. The nature of the organisation is such that it will react to requests for assistance quickly but impose restrictions simultaneously. In time it may be argued that it has failed fully to address the environmental and social impact of the projects it funds. For every dollar it lends more is needed both to service the debt and to defray the costs of a clear-up operation that would have been unnecessary if the project had not begun in the first place.

Throughout 1996 and 1997, Neptune took up a position opposite the eclipse degree of July 1944. It was at this time that endemic problems ballooned. The sheer number of water-based schemes funded by this stage, and the potential for each to be scuppered by difficulties of one sort or another, suggest that the IMF's actions may have been central to the escalating world debt.

The coming years are likely to be difficult for the organisation. It may well have run out of funds and steam before 2008. Neptune opposes the degree held by Mercury at the solar eclipse between 2005 and 2006. Such periods usually coincide with a loss of credibility. It may not be possible to maintain the goodwill that enables the IMF to have funds to lend. A serious crisis looms.

As has been explained, the formation of the planets with the solar eclipse at the time of the IMF's inauguration lay within a 120-degree sector of the zodiac. In August 2001, Saturn crossed the start of this part of the zodiac. Transits of Saturn remind us of the need to acknowledge certain criteria: we become aware of our limitations. This is the second transit of Saturn through this sector since the IMF came into being. Should history repeat itself, then changes in the management structure of the IMF are inevitable.

Even these changes may not be sufficient for those aware that aggregate losses are so great. Only the appointment of a new Chief Executive and total re-formation may be sufficient. This appointment, in 2005, may be extraordinarily difficult to achieve. As has been the case in the past, few people will wish to take on this onerous role. Given the distressed state of the organisation, it could take some months to make the appointment and, even when the appointment is made, to persuade the individual to stay with the task. This too could pave the way for great difficulties in the last years of the decade and beyond.

The Credit Bubble and Currency Collapse

Debt is a growth industry. It is, of course, possible for debt to be managed through philanthropy, where needs are met through managed gift aid, but more commonly debt affords a route by which to manipulate societies. The management of money affords power. It also affords the potential for fraud and corruption. Correlating changes in debt management with the cycles of the planets or weather conditions of the solar system reveals tantalising possible links. Once again, study of the 492-year Neptune–Pluto cycle reveals interesting patterns. Taking this cycle in conjunction with the movement of another planetoid of the solar system through the zodiac, it may even be possible to identify when the present credit bubble will burst.

The last two Neptune–Pluto cycles each began in the sign of Gemini – the sign associated with discourse, trade, commerce and currency. The complexity of activity in these areas has grown phenomenally since 1398.[1] The first of these Gemini-rooted cycles since then saw increased trading through merchant trading ships. The second of the cycles has seen trade expand with the advent of rail, air and motor vehicle travel. Goods that previously would have perished en route from one side of the globe to the other, can now be whisked thousands of miles in hours. Refrigerated lorries then carry the goods quickly to local outlets. What is produced on one side of the world can be made available to the other side in little more than a day. In the case of information traded on the Internet, the same task can be achieved in seconds.

The world has indeed become a global village. A country in one hemisphere can owe extensively to a country in the other. That debt may be paid off in seconds via electronic transfer, or could be spread over several years, incurring costs at the same time. The debt can take on a complexity that would be beyond the understanding of traders of earlier times. Payment may be made in a variety of currencies or in bonds or other products. Quantifying who owes what and to whom has become something of an art form, and has spawned yet another group of traders – those who gamble on the ups and downs of market values.

The most recent Neptune–Pluto cycle began in 1891. Throughout much of the 20th century, Neptune and Pluto were a sixth of a cycle from one another. The sixth-of-a-cycle pattern may be described as a period of controlled and usually harmonious growth. When the aspect was exact, as it was for much of the 20th century, there was a high level of productivity in both the debt and credit industries – yet there was little concern about growth. Generally there was a feeling that 'the books balanced'.

The term creative accountancy can be traced back to the time when the two planets shared a rather different and very much less harmonious aspect. Towards the end of 1986, the two planets moved out of their sixth-of-a-cycle phase. This mathematical relationship between the two will not be seen again until 2026. The intervening years (a near-exact Saturn cycle of 30 years) suggests a period when the two planets may not be 'pulling together'. With neither working with the other, the potential for chaotic activity exists. Credit historians may one day identify the period after 1986 as one when quantifying levels of debt and credit became increasingly difficult. With the inability to assess these levels comes the prospect of chaos.

It is curious to note that it was within months of the two planets moving out of this 'sixth phase' relationship that the electronic age was marked in the City of London with the Big Bang. From this moment the global village market became reality. With share trading now almost instantaneous, a whole new financial world came into being. This event was heralded as a positive development. Historians of the future may take a different view as it becomes accepted that the system required better controls and systems to have been in place before the launch.

It is, obviously, nearly impossible to place controls on instant trading. How could the validity, authority and integrity of every single transaction be checked? How could anyone be sure that the seller owned the goods to be traded or that the buyer held honest funds with which to buy? Following 1986, the time became right for the growth of corrupt activities and for money-launderers to acquire a peculiar professional status.

The movement of drug money can be seen on this same planetary radar screen. Drugs are associated with the planet Neptune (and with the sign of Pisces, to which this planet is said to be affiliated). There are of course good drugs and bad drugs. It has been suggested that some of the larger drug companies manipulate markets in their products to their own financial advantage. Another factor is that illegal drug trafficking is a huge business. Since 1986, despite the best efforts of law enforcement agencies, their influence has not waned and the huge amounts of money involved have not diminished.

Both Neptune and Pluto are a very long way from planet Earth. Astrologers and astronomers are indebted to the gifted individuals working at the Space Agency, NASA, for tables showing the orbits of the two planets. Even with their sterling work, given the distances involved, it is impossible to identify the exact moment when the two planets formed their conjunction (when they appeared to share the same zodiacal position as viewed from Earth). The most up-to-date information indicates that the conjunction could have first been seen on 2 August 1891 and would have been visible with the aid of an appropriately powerful telescope on the eastern horizon just off the coast of Colombia.

Despite the best efforts of its administration, many people view Colombia as one of the main drug-supplying countries of the world. Cocaine and heroin are cultivated on its land. A route frequently used by Colombian traffickers moves north out of the country, across the Bay of Mexico, to Florida and the Bahamian islands. This is almost exactly the line of sight of the Neptune–Pluto conjunction on 2 August 1891. It may be significant too that the conjunction stood proud in the sky over the lower part of Italy and Sicily. The peoples of these two areas of the world appear to have responded particularly to the call of these two planets. A map of the world tracing the apparent movement of these two planets as the Earth turned below them, almost exactly describes the drug-trafficking routes.

Drugs, debt and delusion are natural companions. Each distorts the other. It is probably impossible to assess the full cost of the misuse of drugs – legal or illegal. Debts incurred in the production of drugs of all kinds may similarly be unquantifiable. Whole families are sold into drug slavery either through the growth and harvesting of the product or through the misery of drug-taking family members. The cost – not purely financial – is carried forward from one generation to another.

There is delusion too when the currency used cannot be trusted. The currency of choice for the drug barons has been the US Dollar. Counterfeit dollars have been in circulation for decades with their artistic creators funded by drug barons. The sophisticated machinery at their disposal means that these dollars are virtually indistinguishable from legitimate dollars.

Only electronic eyes can now spot the difference. So, while the level of world debt is given as several hundred trillion dollars, we cannot be sure which of these dollars are valid. World debt is now carried along on its own momentum. The moment of truth has yet to arrive. Indeed, it may not do so until Neptune and Pluto are a quarter of the way through their cycle, in 2061. It is perhaps only at this critical point that the real depth and nature of the problem will be understood.

Credit Bubble Burst

There is another possibility: Chiron,[2] a curious planetoid whose presence was deduced relatively recently (1977), maintains an orbit between Saturn and Uranus. This planet has featured in the sky-patterns apparent at times of financial scandal such as the WorldCom and Enron débâcles. This planetoid's curious orbit results in it spending far longer in some signs than others. At the end of the first decade of the 21st century it will meet with Neptune in Aquarius, and then both bodies will cross over into the next sign, Pisces, in 2013. This synchronicity is unusual. It has not occurred for several centuries. Should it be that Chiron, acting as a cosmic accountant, demands that Neptune, the fraudster and illusionist, face the music at this point, then the collapse of the credit bubble could occur on 17 February 2010. Given the state of the solar system over that year, a very large financial drama seems more than likely. At the very least it seems probable that the early months of 2010 will be critical for various currencies, with the US Dollar experiencing great turbulence.

Currency is just one form of exchange that allows numerous participants to be involved in the movement of services or goods from one person or geographical area to another. It is crucial that the currency used should be accredited at all stages of the exchange process. US dollars are recognised the world over, whilst rupees, rands, sheckels, euros etc. fail to carry the same authority. In days of old, gold, silver and precious jewels served as global currency, as, in some places in the world, they still do.

The US dollar trounces other commodities in its sheer usefulness. The exchange of a handful of dollars for a handful of euros is easily carried out at a bank. Translating a piece of gold or silver into local currency is rather more complicated. It is entirely possible that abuse of the US dollar has been a major contributing factor to the rise in global debt. It is an oft-quoted 'fact' that upwards of 80 per cent of dollars hold traces of cocaine. Whether this is true or not, it surely cannot be disputed that the dollar is the currency of choice for drug barons.

Just as there is no known birth chart for gold, no moment is recognised as marking the birth of the dollar. Even so, analysis of planetary movements over decades enables patterns of trade to be identified. In recent times, the relationship between Neptune and Pluto from several perspectives has assisted in identifying moments of high activity. This cycle alone does not explain the more intricate and, indeed, intra-day price movement.

The movements of the far-faster moving planets Mercury and Venus can be shown to influence currency price movements. Mercury, depicted as the 'winged messenger', orbits the Sun every 88 days, making constantly changing aspects to the other planets. The diverse pictures it creates with the other planets as it travels the sky, permit an image of a deal-maker, incessantly on the move. As it moves from one sign to another – from either the heliocentric or the geocentric perspective – fluctuations in market movements may be seen. Deals that correlate with the movements of the planet Mercury include activity in the commodities markets. Indeed, significant price-change movements may be detected on days when the Sun and Mercury appear together (conjunct) in the sky as viewed from Earth.

Venus moves rather more slowly. Her journey around the Sun requires 225^4 of our Earth days. Again, as she moves from one sign to another – either heliocentrically or geocentrically – price movements occur.

Whereas Mercury trades in ideas and the concept of trade itself, Venus correlates with the most common of base metals – copper. The penny, the rupee, cent and lui to name but a few of the many coins in circulation, are all composed of a base of copper mixed with other metals. These tiny units of currency support, for example, the dollar, the euro and the Swiss franc. Venus, the planet associated with love and pleasure, is also associated with hard cash, so it is no surprise that her movements in the sky correlate with currency price changes.

It is not at all uncommon for periods of turbulence in the currency markets to coincide with eclipse periods and turning points in the Mercury and Venus cycles.

In 1994 astro-economic analysis was used to forecast a currency-market crisis for August 1998. The critical factors here were a solar eclipse in the sign of Leo (associated with gold and possibly indicating movement in that market), coupled with Mercury arriving at a pivotal point in its cycle that same day. The triggering event proved to be a crisis with the Russian rouble that was devalued that same day.[5]

Currency Crisis |

It is not until 15 January 2010 that a near identical picture forms again. This date, just one month ahead of 17 February, the date listed when the credit bubble could burst, at the very least seems likely to mark the start of several weeks of crisis – with enormous repercussions. A solar eclipse in the sign of Capricorn occurs as Mercury reaches a pivotal point in its cycle. Capricorn is an important sign of the zodiac (as it marks a change of season on Earth), so it may be that the developing crisis will be felt worldwide and involve a currency in widespread use. This is unlikely to be the Russian rouble but could possibly be the Euro or the US Dollar. Given the stresses and strains of the year 2010, this currency crisis could be a global disaster that affects the USA, the countries of the Commonwealth, and China and Japan particularly badly.

Whilst this date is likely to witness a serious currency collapse, there are other periods before that date when the currency markets may be said to be precarious. These include 8–12 April 2005, 25–29 May 2006, and 26 January to 1 February 2009. In the following decade, periods to note are 30 December 2010 to 4 January 2011, 24–25 November 2011, 23–25 October 2014, 13–17 September 2015 and 30 August to 1 September 2016.

The US Dollar is likely to be affected by every one of these critical periods. The solar eclipse of 4 December 2002 could be seen as the trigger for a display of dollar turbulence that will last until at least 2020. Indeed, the events of December 2002 may be replayed in December 2019. Before then, the last week of May 2006 would appear particularly difficult. Challenged, those trading the dollar are likely to react wildly to price movements over these few days. The same is true of the period in 2009, and in both periods in 2011, listed above. Over these dates the US is likely to dig deep into its reserves to support the currency.

Eclipse and Mercury-station patterns indicate currency difficulties in the first days of 2011 and again in November of that same year. The Venus declination suggests that gold prices may be poised for action at the start of 2011 – perhaps with increased volume, though not necessarily increased price – but the latter months of 2011 and the start of 2012 point to sharp increases: at the very least meeting the $892 level held in 1980.

In considering the movements of the US Dollar over the next twenty years it is useful to look at the chart for the US Federal Reserve. The 'Fed' came into existence on 23 December 1913[6] and within hours of the Sun's Capricorn ingress. The days on which the Sun moves into any of the

Cardinal signs of the zodiac (Aries, Cancer, Libra or Capricorn) mark those dates when the Sun, in its apparent path around the Earth, comes to a critical phase: these Equinoxes and Solstices have been recognised as powerful dates since time immemorial. Any institution that comes into being on one of these dates may be said to be imbued with extra energy. Since these dates are only relevant to those living on Earth (they are defined by the Sun's relationship to the Earth), they carry special force for human kind.

The Fed's Capricorn energy is very different from that of the International Monetary Fund. If Cancer is the sign of husbandry, then Capricorn is the sign of husbandry and security. Cancer is one of the Water signs of the zodiac. Where Cancer is involved, emotion is never far away. Capricorn, however, is one of the Earth signs and when this sign is involved, practicality is never far behind. Interestingly, Capricorn is the sign most commonly associated with national institutions. There is an implication with national institutions that they will be there to support subsequent generations. Whereas the Cancer trait is to offer support to every family, Capricorn focuses more on the need to support the nation as family.

The Fed is now approaching its centenary. It has coped with many challenges during its existence. If it were a person we might wonder if it were not pathologically driven to prove itself. The chart for its inception shows the Sun at zero degrees Capricorn, opposed by Pluto at zero degrees Cancer. With these two Cardinal points of the zodiac highlighted in such a way, it has super-strong will. The desire to protect itself, at all costs, keeps it alive.

Continually checking that its reserves are not threatened by anyone, it can turn its natural fear of being powerless into the dishonourable trait of using bullying tactics against others. It has been a force to be reckoned with and, prior to the existence of the World Bank, acted as though it had a special mandate to be the centre of the world banking system.

The Fed has been under real pressure in the past and it has recovered. It is not yet old enough to have experienced a transit of Pluto across its Sun and opposite the natal Pluto position, however. Due to the vagaries of Pluto's orbit relative to Earth, this transit occurs no less than five times between February 2008 and October 2009 (the exact dates are 25 February 2008, 10 March 2008, 19 December 2008, 21 August 2009 and 3 October 2009). Intense power struggles both within and outside the Fed suggest that this will be a tense period.

The position of the Sun in the chart of an institution or organisation usually indicates the Chief Executive, Chairman or 'boss'. A transit of Pluto to this solar position suggests both a change of leader and the possibility of aggression towards either the old or the new person. It is common for leaders, during such transits, to talk of coping with 'dirt that's been dug up'. In this instance, given the Sun's natal contact to Pluto, it may be that corruption on a very large scale will be unearthed. Should this be the case, that corruption may well be 'aged' – spanning the better part of the preceding decade.

The Fed differs from the World Bank in that it is acquisitive. Figuratively, the World Bank collects bank drafts whereas the Fed has built up reserves of paper currency and gold. Any threat to the Federal reserves would clearly have an impact on gold prices. Before moving to assess likely changes in the gold price, it may be valuable to show the impact of Alan Greenspan, Chairman of the Fed, on his organisation.

Mr Greenspan[7] was born under the sun sign of Pisces with his Sun closely aligned to the position of the lunar node of the Fed. Some might describe this as a bond of 'fatal attraction'. There is little doubt that Mr Greenspan has been a Captain fully in control of his ship, and one must wonder how stable the ship will be when he has to leave the bridge.

The post-Greenspan era could be very difficult. One of Mr Greenspan's advantages is that he is old enough to have had experience of the deep recession that affected America in the 1930s. His successor may not even have been born then, and whilst this successor would have experienced market crashes and oil price hikes, he would not be able to draw on that same memory bank that has, presumably, enabled Mr Greenspan to keep his ship from hitting the rocks before now.

Those rocks await. The relentless journeys of the planets on their established orbits enable us to identify those periods when the rocks will appear. As seen elsewhere in this book, the latter two years of the first decade of the new millennium come into sharp relief. Will these same years see gold return to the heady heights it held between 1978 and 1981? To know this we have first to assess what was unique about these years.

In the latter part of 1977, the price of gold began to soar.[8] Signals that it was ready to break through its normal ceiling were apparent earlier that year. What eventually occurred was extraordinary. The gold bullion price soared from $280 to $890, dropping back eventually in 1984 to $360. By the autumn of 2002 it had fallen back below $290 with some people feeling that it might never venture off the $300 mark again. It seemed to be a commodity that had fallen out of favour. The Chancellor of the Exchequer in the UK even saw fit to sell off portions of the UK's gold reserves – an action that history may show to have been an error of judgment.

Venus and the Gold Cycle |

To understand what happened to the gold price between 1978 and 1983 it is necessary to look at a different planet cycle. The cycles considered until now have been based purely on any given planet's position relative to zero degrees of Aries. The planets do not, however, travel along precisely the same route. The tropical zodiac can be described as a belt. The planets do not travel along the centre of the belt but have orbits that take them either side of the centre of this belt. Even this is not a uniform wave. On one cycle they may travel to one extreme of this apparent belt and on another perhaps only a part of that distance.

Venus's orbit can take her to an extreme high and an extreme low on this plane. Between 1978 and 1983, this is exactly what occurred. She did not fall back into her usual orbit wave until the mid-1980s — at which time the price of gold fell back into a narrow band. What may have prompted the huge surge in price either side of 1980 was Venus's wild wave, that took her from the upper level of our 'belt' to the lower edge and back again several times in quick succession. This pattern did not appear at any other time in the 20th century. She certainly travelled to those edges but only during this particular time did she visit north and south extremes of declinations within such a tight time frame.

The price shot up wildly in the latter months of 1979,[9] peaking as Venus began a sharp ride to 27 degrees, i.e. maximum declination. A near identical situation occurs between late 2003 and early 2004. Once again the price of gold soared. There are some bumps along the way but generally these high prices are likely to be sustained into 2006. The price will then fall back before we see a repeat performance in 2011 and 2013. Gold may yet prove a safer haven than currencies in the coming decade. The Federal Reserve Board came into being just one short cycle before Venus swung into maximum declination. It is easy to understand how the Board of that day would have deemed it important to hold huge reserves of this precious metal. At the time of writing it is still unknown what those levels might be. We can, however, be fairly sure that they are massive.

As outlined above, planetary trends suggest several crises in the currency markets in the coming years. It is, perhaps, significant that these crises coincide with times when analysis of the Venus declination cycle points to price fluctuations in gold.

Water Wars, 2010

rare planetary alignment takes place in the summer of 2010 when several cycles reach 'critical points'. Just as the Sun and Moon enjoy a relationship which leads from New Moon, to First Quarter, to Full Moon and then Last Quarter Moon, so any two planets enjoy a similar relationship to one another.

In the past, the critical points in the cycles of slow-moving planets have coincided with tension between nations. At the end of this first decade of the 21st century, the extraordinary number of critical points reached during a very narrow time-frame (2008–2011) suggests that tension will be acute. Difficulties within the global community could rise to an extraordinary débâcle – including a furious exchange of military power.

Of course this is by no means inevitable. However, if history does repeat itself, then any one of these important junctures could signal war. It is possible that the cumulative effect of so many cycles reaching critical moments will result in peaceful change in social, political and economic directions. Yet the seeds of violent confrontation could be considered to be in place already. Recent events – particularly in the Middle East – point to the powerful potential for further, deliberate, military action which history may one day describe as World War III.

Various factors other than political ideology – changes in climate, disputes over national boundaries, alterations to natural phenomena (pollution of seas and rivers combined with complex dam structures) – could play an important role. Certainly, the signs of the zodiac, and positions of the planets therein, bolster the argument. The key planets are travelling through Aries, Libra and Capricorn, three of the four Cardinal signs of the zodiac. The missing sign is Cancer, the only one of the four Cardinal signs described also as a Water sign. The cosmos may be sending a powerful message here. This 'missing' component – so essential to life – may become the subject of territorial dispute. Should there be wars at the end of the decade, in time these may become known not as World War III but as the 'Water Wars'.

The extraordinary planet formation actually begins during the autumn of 2008 and within months of another important natural phenomenon. The Moon will have passed closer to the Earth than for some hundreds of years, bringing neap tides – or spring tides – far higher than normal. Flood defences will be seriously tested. However, mankind needs not just plentiful supplies of water, but plentiful supplies of *clean* water. Water agencies across the world will need to have contingency plans in place well ahead of time. (There is concern that the flood barrier on the River Thames in London will not be able to cope. Strengthening and improvement of the Thames Barrier has been delayed, and the required protection levels may not be in place in time. This would put properties in the docklands area of the River Thames at risk.) Débâcle in certain areas of the world could very well lead to the pollution of large areas and, in consequence, increased demand for fresh water supplies.

The planet picture for the period 2008–2011 is decisive. Over this comparatively short period of time, two 'tight-rope' formations of planets form at right-angles to one another. There are periods when tension will be acute, will be released just a little, will become taut again and then will finally reduce as the planets, moving at different speeds, move away from this angular relationship to one another. Indeed, it is possible that from late 2006 there will be talk in many places about the inevitability of global war. Just as analysis of older cycles shows that each phase lays the seeds for later development, it may be that the tensions immediately apparent after the attack on the Twin Towers on 11 September 2001 will not be resolved until critical phases reach intensity at the end of the decade.

Two of the key planetary players in the end-of-decade formation are Saturn and Pluto. The cosmic rhythm of this pair of planets makes fascinating study for the astro-historian. Pluto is the planet associated with deeply-held beliefs, whilst Saturn is the planet associated with structure and government. Throughout the early years of the decade, they lay at opposite sides of the zodiac. When these two planets aspect one another, ancient peoples often find themselves at war with similar peoples who happen to have a different faith or social system.

Throughout the 20th century, this particular cosmic dance has had resonance for the lands and peoples of the Middle East. Disputes between the ancient races of this region have escalated to war within weeks of these two planets reaching important phases in their cycle.

As with any two planets, there comes a time when they appear to lie in a comparative straight line as viewed from Earth: with Saturn and Pluto, this 'line-up' occurs approximately every 35.5 years. During the 20th century, this alignment took place three times: in 1914, 1947 and 1982. Each proved to be an important period in terms of world history. The first, 1914, witnessed the start of what became known as World War I. At the start of the next cycle, in 1947, the State of Israel[1] came into being – a 'birth moment' that has had enormous repercussions on the world's political agenda. In 1982, tension in the Middle East escalated as Israeli boats and planes bombarded Beirut. By September of that year, it was said that Beirut had been plunged into a blood bath.[2] This was not the only area of the world to tune into this cosmic vibration. The apparently unthinkable occurred when Argentina invaded the Falkland Islands, eventually resulting in a war between nations thousands of miles apart.

The space between the 'start moments' or conjunctions of these two planets is rarely peaceful. Indeed, around the times when the planets lie at right angles or oppose one another, similar stress is apparent. Most recently, when the planets reached their 'First Quarter' phase, there were bloody battles – both in Russia, where civil unrest in the early days of October 1993[3] caused anxiety, and in Afghanistan, where it seemed that the country would be torn to shreds by internal factions.

The Israelis and Palestinians reacted differently to this planetary chord, choosing to try to resolve differences whilst acknowledging that if this did not happen, further bloodshed would be inevitable. After a Middle East summit, brokered by President Clinton, the Oslo Accord was signed. Momentarily, at least, it seemed that the violent reaction associated with this cycle had been broken – at least in that part of the world.

Sadly, this peace initiative proved unsustainable. As the two planets moved to oppose one another in the spring of 2001, tension grew once more. This 'Full Moon' phase is often the most critical in any cycle. Just as the Full Moon itself draws emotional reaction to the surface, the Full Moon phase of *any* cycle brings to a head all those issues that are left unresolved. The catastrophic drama of 11 September had yet to unfold at the start of 2001, yet even so, from the spring of that year it was apparent that feelings were running high between nations with diametrically opposed viewpoints. On a number of occasions it seemed that the Middle East was on the verge of war.

82

Nor was this the only region of the world to be affected mid-2001. Tension was growing in the Kashmir region north of India, where aggressive dialogue between Indians and Pakistanis was vividly evident. In Indonesia, fighting was breaking out between groups holding different faiths.

Correlation between tension on Earth and the acute phases of the Saturn–Pluto cycle is compelling – though by no means conclusive. It may be that the last phase of this cycle – due in 2009/2010 – will witness constructive discussion and agreement, but that this time, agreement will be sustainable. However, a peaceful solution and reconciliation cannot be guaranteed. It is more likely that the opposite will be the case and that dramatic confrontation will occur.

Another last phase of this cycle was reached between 15 September 1973 and late May 1974. This proved to be a time of extraordinary difficulty world-wide. On 13 September 1973,[4] within hours of the aspect becoming exact, Israel and Syria fought a horrendous air battle. The violence continued, and whilst this aspect still hung in the sky, Israel countered with the Yom Kippur offensive. Before the end of October 1973,[5] President Nixon had put US forces throughout the world on military alert as fears grew that the Soviet Union would send a substantial force to the Middle East, further inflaming the situation. Nixon's fears proved unfounded and the crisis abated – but not before there had been a flurry of activity, as diplomats globally worked overtime to diffuse the situation. Even so, before the aspect finally dissolved, 16 children died in Arab–Israeli crossfire on 16 May 1974.[6] The deaths of these children, whilst appalling for their communities, were far less than might have been forecast for this planetary formation.

If we look back further, to the last phase of the *previous* cycle, we find ourselves in March 1940. This was a difficult time in World War II. During that month the Red Army finally subdued the Finns,[7] who had defended themselves ferociously. Very early the following month Hitler's armies invaded Denmark and Norway, whilst back in Berlin, Hitler ordered the construction of the first concentration camp.[8] (Hitler[9] was born at another interesting phase in this cycle when the two planets were exactly a seventh of a circle apart from one another. He was clearly in tune with the harsh, authoritarian, cold, ruthless and dark side that is often revealed when Saturn and Pluto reach critical phases in their cycle.)

Recent history suggests that the Last Quarter phase of the Saturn–Pluto cycle tends to connects with periods of brutality on Earth, commonly including the invasion of one country by the armies of another. Should this action recur at the end of the decade, then two other events occurring between November 2009 and the end of 2010 could see the effect amplified. The lunar eclipse on 31 December 2009 may find many people approaching 2010 with apprehension and fear, whilst the Full Moon of 23 September 2010 could coincide with violent action in several theatres of war. Within weeks of both these dates, we might anticipate invasion and catastrophe for some nations.

Technically, the right-angle aspect between Saturn and Pluto is exact in November 2009. However, the two planets will be drawing into this angle for some time beforehand. If we look beyond the aspect and include the movement of Mars (usually seen as the 'God of War') it is possible to find dates when Mars moves into formation between the two slower-moving planets. These days may be viewed as 'red alerts'. Incidents – discussion or action – occurring on these dates, will give clues as to the battles ahead. They include 19 February, 15 April, 12 June and 19 August 2009.

Analysis suggests that the Middle East is particularly responsive to the Saturn–Pluto cycle. The last years of this first decade could, therefore, be difficult for the region. It may not be alone in experiencing problems: astro-geographical[10] techniques are used to identify which capital cities and which areas of the world might be most affected by particular planetary configurations. This area of astrological research has gathered pace since 1977 and is now widely used to identify locations where events might take place. Places on Earth where planets make a prominent appearance seem to be the areas where mankind reacts most strongly to the themes and myths associated with those planets. Saturn and Pluto each take up prominent position over much of Bolivia, the whole of Paraguay and parts of Argentina in 2009. Clashes could occur. Across the world, the peoples of the coast of China and Taiwan might also tune into the harsh vibration of this planet combination.

Perhaps more worryingly, the latitude of the world most likely to be affected is the band a few hundred miles north of the equator. Conditions here could prove exceptionally difficult. This region has already witnessed dark undercurrents of terrorist activity. Further fierce confrontation is possible. At the same time, widespread disease would make the quest for clean and plentiful water even more urgent than normal. Should this region witness feuds of any kind, the escalation of problems would be great – particularly in the autumn of 2010. Given the correlation between world history and this planet cycle, the likelihood of war at the end of this first decade of the millennium cannot be ignored.

The Saturn–Pluto aspect comprises just one unit of the complex planet grouping at the end of the decade. Analysis of another cycle clarifies the picture further.

Within months of Saturn and Pluto reaching their Last Quarter phase, the Uranus–Pluto cycle comes to its 'First Quarter phase'. Further away from the Sun and therefore taking longer to make its orbit, Uranus takes approximately 84 years[11] to complete one revolution around the Sun. As with Pluto, eccentricity is apparent so that there is a wide variation in the time taken from one Uranus–Pluto conjunction to the next. The two planets have enjoyed just eight[12] conjunctions since the year 1000, with the time taken between successive conjunctions varying between approximately 112 and 142 years. There is a rhythm here in that there is relatively greater regularity between alternate conjunctions. This is not a rare feature of synodic periods and may go some way towards explaining why successive cycles do not repeat exactly but, in a sense, 'skip a generation' before repeating the earlier influence. This 'syncopated rhythm' might explain why, when the influences of Uranus and Pluto are felt, there is discomfort, as some people find it harder to adjust to the new rhythm than others.

Uranus, discovered in 1781,[13] is viewed as the 'planet with a difference'. Even astronomers were surprised when the Voyager spaceship's recent encounter showed it to spin on its axis in the opposite direction from the other known planets. Neither did they expect it to have rings, like Saturn. This was a more complex cosmic body than they had anticipated – though astrologers, having studied the effect of the transits of Uranus on their clients' charts, felt vindicated in that this really was the 'planet of surprises'.

Astro-historians have found correlation between times when this planet was in a particular formation and times of shock and change on planet Earth. There are numerous examples: there are no times when the planet is not overhead somewhere on Earth. It was EXACTLY overhead when the first atomic bomb was dropped on Hiroshima.[14] Just four minutes later it would have been above a rather different area. It is unlikely that the Allies figured this information into their planning!

Uranus was in a similarly prominent place when Karl Marx was born, and is often prominently placed in the charts of those who stand out from the crowd in one way or another.

The symbolism linked to Uranus is of revolutionary change. By contrast, Pluto is said to be the planet of regeneration. As the 'God of the Underworld', Pluto is connected with death, decay and destruction before rebirth and transformation.

The vibration created by the mix of these two planets is exemplified by the nature of the generation born around the time of their conjunction alignment. It is possible that these individuals will play an increasingly important role in the coming years. The most recent conjunction of Uranus and Pluto took place between late 1965 and 1966 when both planets were placed in the tropical zodiac sign of Virgo. It would be necessary to trace back to around 3000 BC to find another generation with this positioning of the two planets. It is entirely possible that those born in 1965 and 1966 – and who may be particularly tuned to the frequencies of this particular music of the spheres – will have an important role to play at the end of the decade when the two planets move into their 'First Quarter' phase.

Older generations certainly found the mid-1960s stressful. Mao Tse Tung set a new pace in China with the Cultural Revolution.[16] President Lyndon Johnson sent the Marines into Vietnam *and* into the Dominican Republic.[17] Civil unrest was apparent in the USA when 25,000 people marched in protest in Alabama.[18] In Los Angeles, there were race riots.[19] On the other side of the world, in the sub-continent of India, there were clashes on the Kashmir border. Within months, India and Pakistan were at war with one another.[20] Simultaneously on the African continent, White Rhodesia broke away from Britain,[21] and Nigeria experienced a military coup.[22] Clearly, many governments found this period challenging and chose to react by entering into hostilities.

Those of a more technical and creative frame of mind reacted rather differently. The space-race of this period was fast and furious. Within a year of a Russian astronaut making the first somersault in space, man landed on the Moon,[23] heralding a new age of exploration and discovery – a dramatic development in mankind's understanding of the cosmic environment. Meanwhile, change of a rather different kind was recognized in England, when its capital became known as 'swinging London'.[24]

There are already signs that individuals *born* during this period have unusual qualities. Some have shown extraordinary aptitude for the new technologies, revolutionizing working practices by evolving machines and computers that speed up tasks. Others show rare visual and audio under-standing. From this group we find sound engineers and artists of all kinds who blend their sensitive audio-sensory gifts with understanding and development in robot technologies.

Whilst earlier generations reacted to the meeting of Uranus and Pluto in dramatic ways, we do not yet know how those born in the mid-1960s will react to the First Quarter phase of this cycle at the end of the decade.

Perhaps their ability to 'hear' differently will result in them putting a brake on other generations who feel compelled to take violent action at this time. Perhaps it will be these children of the mid-1960s, frustrated that change isn't happening fast enough, who will be the instigators of such action.

The sheer length of this cycle makes it necessary to sub-divide the cycle even further to gain understanding of the right-angle that will form in a few years' time.

The 'eighth of a circle' phase was reached between March 1986 and December 1987 – a period that encompassed the reactor fire at Chernobyl [25] and the Challenger [26] disaster. These were severe *technical* (a keyword used with Uranus) disasters. The period was eventful in other ways too. Dramatic action took place on a very different stage: political riots occurred in Haiti, South Africa and Pakistan, whilst Iran captured the Iraqi oil port of Faw.[27] Just as the aspect peaked before the two planets edged further away from one another in December 1986, Chinese students led democracy demonstrations across that nation.[28]

The effect is no less dramatic when considering the relationship between the two planets from a different perspective (known technically as 'declination', where the planets involved are equidistant from the ecliptic). This situation occurred in 1975 and coincided with the outbreak of war in both Beirut[29] and Angola.[30] A similar aspect between the two took place in 2002, when hostilities in the Middle East, India, Pakistan and Indonesia again gathered momentum.

Of course it is rare for there *ever* to be prolonged periods of peace in the world. Strife is usually visible somewhere. What seems peculiar to the periods when Uranus and Pluto reach acute phases in their cycle is that the strife takes on more violent and even outrageous proportions and that the political motivation appears to demand a lowering in levels of humanitarianism.

It is, therefore, with some trepidation that we should approach the end of this first decade of the century when the two planets reach their First Quarter phase. This could be an extraordinarily violent time. Nor should we discount the temptation of those in power to use weapons that could bring about mass destruction. The use of these would be entirely in the nature of the combined forces of Uranus and Pluto. Such action would be raw, fast, cruel and uncompromising. Again, it is interesting to look back at times when these two planets were at critical phases in their cycles. Nuclear, chemical and biological weapons may not have been available during these long-gone times, yet appalling events did indeed occur.

This First Quarter phase was reached between 1755 and 1757: a period that encompassed the natural disaster of the Lisbon earthquake[31] and the man-made horrors of the Black Hole of Calcutta.[32] This period also saw the start of the Prussian Seven Years War.[33] More recently, a similar point was reached in 1876/7. This coincided with battles in the Balkans and, in the Americas, the Battle of Little Bighorn and Custer's last stand.[34]

These dates from the past offer little comfort for the future. Once again, if history repeats, there will be great battles on Earth that mirror the tension in the sky created by the right-angle alignment of Uranus with Pluto.

If Saturn is in Last Quarter phase with Pluto during this period, and Uranus is in First Quarter phase with Pluto, then Saturn and Uranus must be at their Full Moon – or opposition – phase. Saturn, the easily identified planet with the rings, will be at one side of the zodiac while Uranus, the planet whose eccentric astronomical features endow it with maverick-type tendencies, lies at the other side. The tug-of-war between these two planets occurs approximately every forty-five years and coincides with struggles between old and new political movements.

The Full Moon, or opposition phase, of the Saturn–Uranus cycle occurred just twice in the 20th century. Both periods proved politically and economically decisive. The first occurred in 1918 at the end of World War I. This was a period of extraordinary social, economic and political upheaval. The map of Europe was changed virtually overnight. The attitude of the soldiers returning from the trenches secured a new wave of political thinking whilst, economically, dramatic changes took place. Whether for good or ill, the pace of change was fast.

The other 20th century opposition of these two planets took place between 1965 and 1967 – a period already noted for upheavals and, in some areas, high levels of violence. 'Upheaval', 'rebellion' and 'overthrow' come from the vocabulary of Uranus and Pluto. Saturn's language is different. Saturn's presence in the configuration brings those challenges to the seat of existing government. Existing rules and regulations are challenged. New methods of working – often created by the incorporation of new technology – demand different types of legislation and make certain working practices obsolete. Entrenched positions become subject to scrutiny. The more obstinate of politicians tend to polarise under this pressure resulting in fierce dialogue. Ultimately this takes the form of battles between conservative die-hards, who apparently oppose progress, and those whose love-affair with a new age blinds them to the value of older methods of working. The Saturn–Uranus opposition often manifests as political challenge and is felt most acutely in regions of the world where the configuration is positioned directly overhead or on the horizon.

Viewed from Earth this aspect takes place no fewer than five times between early November 2008 and late July 2010. The fact that the aspect appears to occur so many times in nearly two years is due to our geocentric perspective. Both the Earth and the planets are on the move and so, from the geocentric perspective, the aspect can take place more than once in the course of some months. During this period the planetary tight-rope formation shifts from one zodiac axis (Virgo–Pisces) to another (Libra–Aries). The fact that so many signs are involved is important. Different nations tend to be more affected by activity in certain signs than others. With four signs of the zodiac affected, there is potential for many countries to be involved. The oppositions of the 20th century accented just one axis on each occasion. To use the musical analogy once more, this time we have three cymbal crashes followed by two notes on large gongs. A great many people will hear – and presumably respond – to these notes.

Of particular interest are those nations known to have a bias towards the Cardinal signs of the zodiac. Within this group[35] we find the United States of America, the United Kingdom, China, Russia and France (all the countries of the present United Nations Security Council). Furthermore, Australia, Canada, Germany, Saudi Arabia, Pakistan, Argentina, Venezuela, Afghanistan, Nigeria and Indonesia, amongst others, are likely to be affected. Each of these nation states is likely to experience political challenge and upheaval.

Of course political upheaval and challenge does not necessarily lead to war. But, as we have seen above, the opposition between these two planets occurs at a time of stress elsewhere in the zodiac and such tension could well be mirrored on Earth.

Elsewhere in this book, and of particular interest to the economist, there is mention of the Jupiter–Saturn cycle. This cycle also reaches a peak in the latter years of the decade. As with the Saturn–Uranus mix, it too affects four signs. The first opposition occurs in May 2010 and the last on 28 March 2011 (as viewed from Earth).

This cycle is far shorter than those mentioned earlier. These two planets meet every 20 years. Astrologers of old gave great credence to this cycle. Until 1781 and the discovery of Uranus, these two planets marked the outer edges of the known solar system. They were known as the rulers of the ages, or Great Chronocrators. The astro-historian is able to trace developments in European social history with the phases of this cycle. During the 20th century the opposition phase of this cycle was reached five times. On each occasion the political and social map of Europe underwent change.

As the largest of the known planets, Jupiter has acquired a reputation for exaggeration and largesse. By contrast, Saturn is associated with controlled order. It is hardly surprising that when the two planets pull against one another there is evidence of rising nationalism. This was certainly true in Europe during the period 1910–1911 and later in 1930–1931. Similar evidence may be seen in both Britain and in Egypt in 1951 and 1952. Rather different types of nationalism were witnessed at the next opposition, in 1970, when France mourned the death of Charles de Gaulle, whilst in Poland a new social order was developing as anti-government riots took hold.

The very last of the 20th century oppositions of these two planets was no less dramatic. Towards the end of the 1980s, Saturn was joined in the sign of Capricorn by both Uranus and Neptune. This pattern had last occurred in the late 14th century. In 1989, Jupiter moved into position at the opposite point of the zodiac and there was huge upheaval culminating in dramatic displays of people power – not all of which were successful, of course. Even so, the collapse of the old Soviet empire, the unification of East and West Germany, not to mention the ending of apartheid and the emergence of a new South Africa, changed the world order significantly.

Planet cycles rarely repeat exactly; more commonly there are 'variations on a theme'. In 2010, Jupiter will oppose Saturn as it did in 1989 and 1990. This time, however, Pluto replaces Neptune in the planetary picture. Neptune, a large gaseous planet of swirling mists, is associated with the dissolution of structures and ideology. It is, perhaps, thanks to the presence of this planet in the earlier planet formation that the Berlin Wall simply 'gave way'. Sadly, the peaceful protestors in Tiananmen Square suffered a dreadful fate at around the same time. Even so, it is generally acknowledged that a new world order came into being relatively peacefully.

It is most unlikely that the same will be true at the end of this decade. Pluto – whose position in the configuration of the decade warrants careful attention – has a reputation for dramatic intervention, often even using the cleansing methods of death and destruction. A painful transition to another new age seems likely in 2010. With Jupiter, the planet of excess, also involved, we might describe the transition as potentially 'extremely painful'.

The ancients noted that types of energy associated with each planet could be observed more clearly when the planets were moving through particular sectors of the zodiac. For example, Pluto appears to work more obviously, perhaps even efficiently, when moving through Scorpio rather than through the opposite sign of Taurus. In assessing the end-of-decade configuration, the affinity of the planets and signs involved permits further insights into difficulties ahead. As mentioned earlier, the very fact that the Water element is missing suggests that water itself could have a more than usually vital role to play.

Defining that role may be done in two ways. It is a fact that life on Earth cannot continue without adequate and plentiful supplies of clean water. Without this, disease becomes rife. If water were to be used as a tool to manipulate nations, then war would be an inevitability. There is another option which could be as powerful. For much of the 20th century, oil proved to be the 'new gold'. A replacement energy system could yet be found. If this took the form of cold fusion requiring vast quantities of pure water, then once again there would be reason for some nations to fight against others for the rights to this commodity.

On a more positive note, there is every reason to suppose that the last few years of the decade will witness exciting technological breakthroughs. These often resonate with the Jupiter–Uranus cycle. This cycle reaches a new start point during this period. Earlier cycles coincided with the race to put man in space and then man on the Moon. Further expeditions across the wide frontier of space would seem likely at the end of the decade. However, if, on this occasion, developments in space experiments were to lead to a further scientific breakthrough on Earth that required water as a catalyst or component, once again there would be reason to fight for access to water supplies.

The time-frame for potential conflict seems clear. The first of the aspects of this powerful formation occurs on 4 November 2008 (from the geocentric perspective). There is minor relief to the tension of this aspect on 21 November of that same year. Thereafter, however, there is a squall of difficult aspects that run throughout 2009 and 2010, and are not relieved until July 2011. This entire period should be seen as potentially stressful and violent.

The cosmos provides a sophisticated method for identifying geographic hot-spots. Solar eclipses occur at least twice, if not five times, in any year. They are not always total; neither may they be seen from every place on Earth. As the Moon's shadow appears to move over the face of the Earth, darkness falls. The number of minutes taken for the effect to clear has relevance. Of course, the longer the eclipse takes, the more likely it is to be seen by many – as, due to the Earth's constant turning, the eclipse will come into view over a great many miles of the Earth's surface. The theory has been that the longer the eclipse, the greater the impact. History suggests that this is indeed the case and that those eclipses which have been seen by many have coincided with periods of great change on Earth, and, it could be argued, that those changes have been most obviously seen in the geographic areas covered by the eclipse.

The solar eclipse that takes place on 22 July 2009 carves a path from the west coast of India all the way across South-East Asia towards Shanghai. That same day, Venus and Saturn lie at apparent right-angles to one another. In India, around the time of the eclipse, Venus will be proud in the sky. This implies that India is likely to play a major role in any dispute and that many of its citizens could find themselves caught up in the débâcle. The next solar eclipse, on 15 January 2010, will again be visible from Southern India and across South-East Asia, concluding its path of visibility in China south of Beijing.

India gained independence on 15 August 1947 [36] – as did its neighbour, Pakistan. Critical points in planet cycles affected both countries more or less simultaneously (there is a small variation in the starting points of each horoscope, reflecting the positions of the capital cities of the two countries). Comparison of the position of the planets in 1947 with their position through 2009 and 2010 suggests that both countries might be in a confrontational frame of mind. The history of the last half-century suggests that military action could be taken by both countries. In this instance, events could be dramatic and affect the lives of many millions of people.

Should the rulers of China be true to their national horoscope (based on 1 October 1949) they too may be in belligerent humour in the summer of 2009 – most especially in July of that year. By the time of the solar eclipse of January 2010, an even uglier mood could take hold. Again, unless the Chinese government breaks with its behavioural pattern as identified through planet cycles, we should expect the Chinese military to be at war early that year. Nor should we discount the countries that lie between these two great nations: Nepal, Burma, Bangladesh, Bhutan, Pakistan and Afghanistan. In each and every case, the potential for involvement in struggle is apparent.

Indonesia too should be singled out for possible involvement. An earlier solar eclipse, on 26 January 2009, is visible from most of those islands and coincides with considerable tension across their basic planet pattern (horoscope). The situation in this part of the world could be particularly violent.

Indonesia in its present form came into being in December 1949 – just a few weeks after the 'birth' of modern China. Symbolism of the unity of a group of islands under one common flag is apparent from its inception. That unity appears under threat in May 2009 particularly – though this is unlikely to come as a surprise to many. A build-up of political tension in this region may be traced back over several decades. Even so, the pressure for change and, potentially, for the collapse of the state, is great during the first half of 2009.

Neither should the 'dark continent' be neglected in this short appraisal. The solar eclipse of January 2010 becomes visible in the south of Nigeria and cuts across the African continent before sweeping up towards the south of India and on into South-East Asia. Genocide has occurred in these areas before. This time, the ruthlessness of certain factions could be appalling. The displacement of large numbers of people and the lack of facilities to feed and clothe them will contribute to epidemics. Under these conditions it is easy to see that the need for water – fresh, clean and plentiful – will play a crucial role.

10 Illusions and Imagination

Imagining the future is a challenge that can be much assisted by understanding what is happening in the cosmos. We know that mankind's view of the heavens changes over the years as both the stars and planets appear to move around the Earth. The astro-historian finds correlation between this changing view and developments in the world of science. As the slower planets move from one part of the zodiac to another, ideas incubate – generally surfacing through the genius of particular individuals. Einstein's Theory of Relativity was presented to the world in 1915, as Uranus moved through Aquarius – the sign in which its influence appears particularly marked. Advances in scientific thinking are common during this transit.

As Uranus returned to this area of the zodiac in the late 1990s, several exciting scientific breakthroughs took place – amongst these, a rapid development in understanding of the human genome and successful developments in cold fusion experiments. Both these and other scientific breakthroughs suggest that, once again, Uranus's transit through this area of the zodiac has coincided with new understanding.

However, to arrive at these achievements it has first been necessary for someone to *imagine*. The quest for greater understanding comes as a result of thinking differently. While the final burst of original thinking and subsequent breakthrough correlates, in these instances, with Uranus's movement through Aquarius, it is the movement of other planets that stimulate the imagination. Indeed it may be that, at a later time, it will be recognised by scientists that 'Energy follows Thought'. As yet, appreciation of this important concept is still in its infancy.

The mind is infinitely more complex than previously understood. Important breakthroughs have been made in understanding dreams and in what takes place in the first minutes after awakening. We know too that lunar phases play a role, with the quality and clarity of dreams varying according to this important physical cycle. It now appears that the position of the planets and the interaction between their cycles plays a profound role in our thought patterns also. If this is the case, and we can decode at least some of these, we may be better placed to avoid decision making during times of cosmic disease and maximise our potential at times of cosmic harmony. Developing the power of the mind and choosing times and specific locations for experiments according to cosmic influences could be key factors in the coming years.

Early in the 1950s, an article was commissioned by a national newspaper. The writer was asked to imagine the world in 2000. Much of what was imagined did indeed become reality. One person had used his imagination together with known scientific developments to suggest what might be achieved within a given time-frame. *The Financial Universe* purports to do the same but uses the code of an ancient language to access the future. Whereas the newspaper writer was attempting to do the literary equivalent of climbing a wall without assistance, *The Financial Universe* aims to show that using awareness of cosmic energies and planet cycles offers 'rungs' and time-frames whereby the shape of the future can be better determined and reacted to.

Observation of the movement of the planet Neptune, both through the zodiac itself and in relation to the other known planets, suggests links between this movement and developments in human imagination.

The early film-makers 'imagined' futuristic vehicles that would transport man into space. It was not so long before those theatrical spaceships became reality. The imaginative efforts finally resulted in something tangible and practical. The efforts of human imagination are a prerequisite to effecting change or creating a new world. If we could not imagine a world free of disease, then efforts to eradicate viruses and genetic misprints would not find favour.

We live in exciting times. The pace of change has been fast in recent years. This may, in part, be due to the extraordinary activity on the sun's surface, which has, perhaps, affected each and every one of us, lighting creative fires within our psyches. It may also have something to do with the position of Neptune in relation to the tropical zodiac. This extraordinary planet is often involved in the planet formations apparent at moments of inspiration and creativity of a very high order.

Neptune began its journey through Aquarius in 1998. It will be 2011 before the planet makes its Pisces ingress, and 2025 (past the limits of this book) before it crosses the threshold of Aries. To recap: the tropical zodiac is a simple division of the Sun's apparent path (the ecliptic) into twelve equal-sized zones. These may be viewed as similar to the twelve notes of a musical octave. As any planet moves from one sign into the next, a modulation of sorts takes place, as if it is moving to a different key, just as music has an effect on the human ear, and human responses. It is interesting, then, for the astro-historian to look back on earlier transits of a planet through a sign to evaluate any apparent influence.

Neptune last visited Aquarius in 1834, leaving that sign in 1847. It was not until 1845, just as Neptune was coming to the end of its Aquarius transit and about to enter Pisces, the sign with which it is said to have greatest affinity, that the planet was discovered or rediscovered (there is a growing body of opinion that believes the ancients were aware of the planets Uranus, Neptune and Pluto, but that this knowledge was lost). Neptune has now made a complete orbit of the Sun since its 'discovery'.

Neptune's emergence (or re-emergence) into world consciousness was unusual. Two mathematicians, one in Cambridge, the other in France, simultaneously declared its presence. Confusion as to who exactly did 'find' it remains to this day. It is in keeping with the astrologer's understanding of Neptune's vibration that this should be the case. Nothing ever seems clear when this planet is involved. It appears to operate on a plane beyond human language and even, perhaps, beyond the limits of our understanding. Just as it is hard to quantify the value of Art, the precise timing even of the planet's discovery is elusive. Neptune seems to be associated with both intangibles and imponderables. The glyph used by astronomers and astrologers for this planet is a trident – appropriate for this 'God of the Sea'. Yet it might just as easily be a question mark. If Neptune has any relevance for human behaviour it is in seeking answers and meaning in the most confusing of situations. As we know, the sea itself is hard to describe. Its texture, quality and mineral properties are varied. We know that the seas are pulled by the tides yet the actual extent of their influence is, again, variable. The sea can be particularly and surprisingly erosive. Yet it can also be a great provider of energy.

Both Uranus and Pluto may have entered world-consciousness amid fanfares; the existence of Neptune took rather longer to accept. Though Neptune was discovered in 1845,[1] it was many months before the world was ready to acknowledge this 'addition' to the solar system. By the time Neptune's presence was accepted, the planet was just beginning to make its passage through Pisces – the sign of the fishes and the sign to which, it is said, it has closest affiliation.

Neptune, like the lager advert, is said to 'reach the parts others cannot reach'. It 'rules' the sea and water. Anyone who has ever experienced a major leak in their home knows that water seeps into unimaginable places, creating extraordinary havoc that takes an age to eradicate. In areas where there has been flooding there are watermarks indicating the levels reached by the rising water – presumably each inundation started with just a few drops of water before developing into a catastrophe. A drop of rain does not necessarily become a flood, and there is a certain amount of mystery involved in predicting whether a downpour will turn into something more dramatic or not.

In astrological terms, Neptune is linked with anything that cannot be contained or quantified. It has associations with the insurance industry, where the scale of potential disaster is often unclear, and with media industries, where the effect of an advertising campaign may be hard to quantify. More recently, it has been said to have an affiliation with the Internet. This extraordinary network seems to know no limits and enables information to encircle the globe at phenomenal speed, incurring negligible cost, and to arrive at unknown destinations on unmonitored screens to be viewed by an anonymous audience. It is at present impossible for any individual placing material on the 'web' to know where and by whom it will be viewed.

The world-wide-web (www) was the brain-child of university dons who wished to exchange information with one another. Their ideal solution to the communications difficulty was to create a system that allowed easy access at all times of the day and night and from many locations. It is very appropriate that the concept came into being while Neptune was working its creative magic in the sign associated with universities and communications over distance, Sagittarius.

It is equally understandable that some of these individuals were slow to realise its commercial possibilities. With the exception of a few, these professors were more interested in the exchange of information rather than the business opportunities that would be provided by the Internet. These would become apparent as Neptune moved on into the business-orientated sign of Capricorn.

Equally, these same individuals were slow to relate to the Internet's potential for attracting those who derive pleasure from creating mayhem. Information and misinformation distributed through the Internet is available to everyone with a modem, keyboard and phone line. On the positive side, this electronic distribution service brings unparalleled, quality information to many. Negatively, those same electronic tendons carry viruses and other corrupting material.

The explosion of both positive and negative activity on the Internet fits neatly with Neptune's passage through the Air-sign of Aquarius. Neptune reached this sign in 1998 and will enjoy a 13-year stay. The Internet will no doubt expand exponentially during this time, as will email and advertising traffic. By the time Neptune concludes its Aquarius odyssey the world really will seem to be a global village.

Interestingly, Aquarius is viewed as the most 'political' of all the signs of the zodiac. Individuals born under this sign often have strong opinions and enjoy having these challenged. Those who are particularly Aquarian (those whose charts show them to have been born when several planets were grouped in this sign) provoke discussion and enjoy debate. For these people, every opinion has value. Aquarius people do not tolerate discrimination and would certainly baulk at the idea that any group could buy their way into power. The Internet provides an extraordinary vehicle for a new wave of political thinking. It is now possible for like-minded people right across the globe to join forces and to arrange global demonstrations.

In the coming years, this type of political movement is likely to grow exponentially as more and more people come on line. By the time Neptune leaves Aquarius in 2011, the political landscape is likely to have changed forever. Even the smallest of voices will carry the same weight as those who have considerable funds at their disposal. It will be possible for someone with very little funding, but considerable creative flair, to achieve high office.

In the world of Art, Neptune's Aquarius vibration is already at work. Media directors, most notably Michael Moore in the United States, have delivered powerful political messages in colourful, dramatic documentaries. This merging of art with politics looks set to continue. The pace could gather further with advancement in home entertainment systems. Since Neptune's Aquarius ingress, wide-screen televisions have grown more popular. By 2011 it is hard to imagine that many of the old screen systems will be left in use. The days of 3D home television may not be far away. Then again, one sense that has not been catered for in this fast-developing world is that of smell. Perhaps, as Neptune moves from Aquarius into the extra-sensory sign of Pisces, provision for the stimulation of this sense via home-entertainment systems will be made.

In art itself, we should anticipate the development of new uses of colour.

With new chemical techniques evolving, so too may new colours and shapes move into the popular domain. Air brushing, air-quality and air movement (all keywords associated with Aquarius) will increasingly intrude on personal consciousness. Eventually, however, the pop-up advertising campaigns of the present time are likely to evolve into subliminal advertising methods, as Neptune moves on into Pisces.

Fascinating parallels can be found too between the development of musical thought and Neptune's journey through the twelve signs. Neptune's Aquarius passage in the 19th century witnessed fast development in the Wind family of instruments. The bassoon, which had been evolving for some time, became a more reliable instrument thanks to the work of the German designer Heckel.[2] Composers of the day found the instrument intriguing. It offered them a platform to extend the tenor and bass lines within the orchestra. In this technical age, the new instruments are electronic but, as before, are extending the range and pitch qualities available to the composer.

Neptune is also closely linked with the pharmaceutical industry. If Neptune influences our senses through the Arts, drugs perform a similar feat. The merging of some of the larger drug companies as Neptune moved through the sign of Capricorn (large corporations) in the 1990s resulted in the tentacles of this industry, just as with the Internet, reaching hitherto isolated regions of the world. Whether in the quest for new drugs or in treating suffering, these large conglomerates have penetrated vast areas of the world and have had enormous impact.

Having established a global presence, these companies are well placed to pursue new drugs to incorporate into their product inventories. Priority is likely to be given to the development of drugs that influence the brain. Reducing brain fatigue and mental stress as well as developing drugs that decrease the incidence of depression and psychotic illness sets the tempo for these companies and is likely to be the area in which they achieve greatest success before 2011. With a growing number of people falling prey to mental illness, demand for hospitals and care centres to look after the needs of those suffering in this way is marked. Pharmaceutical firms are likely to be successful too in developing products that reduce the effects of ageing.

It is unwise to look at one planet's journey in isolation. Whilst Neptune's odyssey through Aquarius and Pisces is interesting, interaction with Uranus's orbit around the Sun provides further food for thought. From 2003 to 2009 there is a curious rapport between these two planets. This affinity is similar to that experienced in the 19th century. The eight years between 1835 and 1843 were extraordinary. Of particular interest to the astro-economist is that there was a significant financial crisis in England and Ireland in 1836.[3] Should history repeat itself, then 2004 and 2005 should be seen as financially precarious for these regions.

Even a cursory appraisal of developments in the field of science during this earlier period suggests that if the influence is repeated, then the next few years will be fascinating. In 1836 Faraday discovered self-induction of a coil of wire;[4] he had written his Electrostatic Induction and Specific Induction Capacity and experimented on the polarisation of light. The German meteorologist Heinrich Dove found that polar and equatorial air-streams had a major influence on European weather;[5] Samuel Morse[6] of the United States developed the telegraph; Charles Goodyear[7] began india-rubber vulcanisation; Christian Doppler[8] proposed a change of wavelength caused by the relative motion of source and observer; and Crawford Long[9] first used an anaesthetic in an operation. Each of these developments were to have enormous impact in the succeeding years and each bears a strong relation to the mythology and attributes associated with the two planets moving in tandem through particular sectors of the zodiac.

From the purely economic perspective, each of these major advances would go on to have a profound effect on the profit margins of companies associated with them — although it may be said that it took some years for this to come about. The scientific and technical breakthroughs made during the years 2003 to 2008 may also require a few years for testing and analysis before they too bring rewards to investors.

Following the eventful period at the end of this first decade, needs are likely to change. Indeed, by the time Neptune makes its Pisces ingress, the desperate need to find drugs to combat the scourges of Aids, malaria, diabetes, cancer, cholera and diphtheria could take on new urgency. Whilst we should anticipate breakthroughs in the understanding of these diseases prior to 2011, the development of treatment programmes for these diseases should gather pace after that time. Indeed, the very centres that are used primarily for the treatment of mental illness in the first decade of the 21st century could be transformed into centres for healing these diseases during the second decade. In this instance, the value of clean, adequate and partic-ular types of water supply takes on fresh meaning.

Coinciding with the latter stages of Neptune's journey through Aquarius, alarm at the effects of radiation — through the use of mobile phones and traffic navigational systems — could give way to changes in the way these devices can be operated. There are also likely to be health forums discussing how the brain can be better protected from this form of pollution.

We should not forget that it is before the end of this first decade that sun-spot activity is due to reach a minimum. A reduction in the number of sun-spots has, in the past, increased human creativity. Should that creativity also be linked to Neptune's presence in Aquarius, technological and bio-chemical advances could be considerable.

Indeed, from late 2006 and all the way through to 2009 the rate of breakthroughs might even give birth to a whole new sector. As with the 'dot-coms' of the 1990s, these 'brainwave companies' could have huge and near immediate success. The seeds of intuitive technology are likely to be sown during Neptune's Aquarius journey, and should grow quickly. Already the advent of video mobile phones and their widespread use is attracting considerable attention and will, inevitably, have a huge impact on daily life. Growing use of 'iris technology' as a means of personal identification is destined to have extraordinary impact also. At present there is still a degree of anonymity about the Internet, in that it can be hard to identify the originator of any single email. However, the last few years of this first decade could see the advent of computers that recognise their owner through iris identification and use this information to authenticate messages sent.

Of course, by the time Neptune enters the sign of Pisces in 2011, intuitive technologies will no longer be seen as unusual or innovative. Just as both refrigerators and televisions were quickly adopted as basic items of furniture, various items falling under the umbrella of intuitive technology will become the norm. These items are likely to become more aesthetically pleasing after 2011 as people tune in to a very different vibration.

The most positive and dramatic effect of Neptune's Pisces passage is likely to be changes in attitudes to healing. It is not improbable that the period 2011 to 2025 will witness the gradual winding-down of the type of hospitals with which we are familiar and the invasive surgical approaches they provide. These are likely to give way to the development of healing sanctuaries that make full use of the power of the mind to alleviate disease.

Space has been described as the 'final frontier'. Yet it may not be space, but knowledge of the inner-workings of the brain that excites mankind from 2011. Neptune last visited the sign of Pisces between 1847 and 1861. This was a time of profound change in attitude to healing generally. Understanding of the properties of ether permitted the first use of anaesthesia, whilst another chemical, nitro-glycerine, came to be used in the treatment of angina pectoris.[10] Other medical developments taking place during this earlier transit of Neptune through Pisces included the appointment of a chief medical officer for London. Mr John Simon[11] created a public health service that would come to be envied. This same period saw the science of epidemiology established. It soon became understood that environmental conditions could influence the spread of disease.

Mention was made previously of the growing body of scientific opinion concerning the influence that the experimenter has on the outcome of an experiment. Neptune's next Pisces odyssey could see this rule expand considerably. It may be that the mental state of a patient will be given due and acknowledged consideration before a programme of healing is begun. The value of positive thought and the use of drugs to promote this state of awareness may be used progressively in the treatment of disease.

Whereas Neptune's earlier journey through Pisces coincided with attention being given to physical cleanliness, after 2011 considerable care and attention may be given to overall environmental conditions – as in the use of colour, sound and smell. Equally, water with newly defined properties is likely to demand greater attention.

It was during the earlier transit that the second law of thermodynamics[12] gained authority, and 1848 when the absolute scale of temperature[13] was determined (later to be known as the Kelvin scale). The transfer of heat from one place to another is also going to become important in the coming years. Experiments in cold fusion have already achieved some success. Following Neptune's entry into Pisces we should expect to hear more of this energy source. With declining oil stocks, this development could have a profound effect.

When Neptune last made its way through Pisces, the existence of mineral deposits in the form of oil was discovered. Developments in this industry correlate almost exactly with the planet's journey through the zodiac. Early in the next decade, Neptune will be almost back at the place it held when oil was first discovered.[14] It is already known that oil stocks will be inadequate post-2020. It remains to be seen if an alternative source of energy will come to the fore ahead of this potential crisis. Developments in cold fusion techniques afford just one possibility. Another will be to harness the not inconsiderable powers of the sea and tidal forces. Whilst this has been done to a limited extent, advances in these areas could effect dramatic change on the balance of the economies of the world.

In 1859, cocaine was first isolated from the leaves of the coca plant,[15] to produce an anaesthetic. Around the same time Louis Pasteur showed that some micro-organisms cannot survive in the presence of air.[16] The rapid development of bio-chemistry in the 19th century may well be mirrored in the 21st century as new drugs are developed. Perhaps more importantly, the manner in which these drugs are administered will come under close scrutiny. The move towards ensuring that the 'right' person administers these at the 'right' time and in the 'right' place is likely to gather pace.

The use of drugs provides just one method in the quest for an altered state of consciousness. Such a state can also be achieved through trance and the experience of religious visitation. Bernadette of Lourdes experienced her great vision (11 February 1858) during Neptune's earlier transit of Pisces. Further similar and important visitations could occur after 2011 as Neptune once again moves through this sign. Greater awareness of the needs and gifts of others is likely to emerge after 2013. On one level, acts of charity should increase. On a very different level, the essence of each person is likely to gain greater respect.

Already there has been much discussion as to the difference between mind and spirit. Greater understanding of the latter is likely before 2020, whereas better understanding of the workings of the mind will be apparent in the years to 2011. We should anticipate that developments in these areas will be dramatic. Even so, they may not be sufficiently dominant to avert catastrophe in some areas of the world during the last years of the first decade.

Cutting Edge

The relationship between the planets and their position in the zodiac relative to Earth provides one platform for forecasting. Historical analysis of these repeating cycles affords a means of determining which areas of human interest and behaviour will surface during specific periods. These cosmic rhythms are ancient – though each generation's response to the patterns and pulse of the sky varies a little from that of a preceding one. History never quite repeats. These cosmic rhythms syncopate. The unexpected then occurs, requiring rapid adjustment to plans. It is hardly surprising that some decisions later prove ill-judged. The enchantment with which new developments are greeted is all too often replaced by deep concern that we are 'playing with fire'. Inherent dangers that accompany new developments may not be understood until too late. Under such conditions it is easy for us to fall into 'crisis management' mode; yet we cannot 'put the genie back in the bottle'. So it is that with each new age, mankind is challenged to find expressions of creativity that can be incorporated with minimum angst. For example, the benefits of splitting the atom must be weighed against the inherent dangers.

Analysis of the movements of Uranus through the various sectors of the zodiac gives clues as to the types and style of discontinuity that might occur. Requiring approximately 84 of our Earth years to circumnavigate the Sun, Uranus will move through the signs of Pisces (2003–2010), Aries (2010–2015) and Taurus before the year 2020. These areas of the cosmic dance-floor offer new possibilities for Uranus's tap-dance. As it moves from one sign to another, mankind is challenged to adjust to a new beat.

The rhythm of Uranus, the planet most associated with revolutionary thinking, is punctuated by sounds associated with technically advanced machinery. Accelerated developments in technology affect corporate structures by reducing the need for certain types of workers and increasing the need for those skilled in new systems. The hum of these new machines replaces the sounds of an earlier age. A new rhythm emerges – at once comforting to owners as labour costs are cut, and alien to workers who are unfamiliar with the new technology, and who indeed may be displaced by it. Yet these new systems spawn new industries too. In the closing years of the 20th century, as Uranus passed through Aquarius, whole new service industries grew as companies sought outside assistance for the technical maintenance of their recently acquired computing and networking systems.

The impact of each planet as it sweeps through the sectors of the zodiac varies. Correlation between activity on Earth and these journeys is not consistent. Some planets appear to have a greater effect in some segments of the zodiac than in others. Uranus's Aquarius odyssey has tended to produce an odd sensation on Earth. It is as though time itself has 'speeded up' – Aquarius is, after all, one of the 'Air' signs of the zodiac. As Uranus moves through this sector of the zodiac, a collective brain-storm occurs. New gadgets appear and there is a thirst to bring new solutions to old problems. The possibility of improvement is seductive. Few can resist the pull towards these new developments. Investors particularly are keen to 'get in at the ground floor'. The human brain is challenged to learn new skills; from mastering the technology of a new video-cam to remembering pin-numbers for a security system, minds are challenged. Pressure to make use of new products and services can deflect certain questions. Few dare ask if the world is really better off by incorporating these ideas. Uranus is a demanding drummer and, for the most part, it is easier to yield to its beat than to resist. It is only as the beat changes (with the planet's move into the next zodiac sector) that we may realise that we have danced with the devil and that we need to slow down and assess the havoc created by scientific and technological developments. Our emotions will most certainly need time to catch up.

Uranus's Pisces advent (2003) has brought with it a wave of developments in biochemistry. Whilst some of these developments will spur the eradication of some diseases or could facilitate greater crop yields, these are early days. The risk-management factor has yet to be fully assessed, and some of the research being carried out is being hotly debated – often under the guise of science versus religion. This is an unusual development at this point in the cycle. Doubt about recent developments usually begins as Uranus moves on into the *next* sign. The present period is different – perhaps because of a most unusual displacement.

A constant theme throughout the previous chapters is that the planets appear to work rather better in some signs than in others. A curious feature of the present time is that Uranus is moving through a sector preferred by Neptune, and Neptune is moving through one preferred by Uranus. This overlapping condition will last from 2003 to 2010 – the latter date marking the time when Uranus moves on into the sign of Aries. At this point there is a discontinuity. Given the other factors applying at the end of the first decade, this could yet prove to be a most difficult year indeed for mankind. It is perhaps only at this point of discontinuity that truly negative influences will be fully apparent. It is, perhaps, in 2010 that we will all wish that we could put certain genies back in their bottles.

Between 1835 and 1843 (the last time this curious symmetry between Uranus and Neptune occurred), the pace of change was, as now, fast and imaginative yet bewildering – just as it had been between 1670 and 1675 when the two planets enjoyed a similar relationship. In 1671, Leibnitz described the existence of the aether. In 1839, Theodor Schwann laid the foundations of cell growth theory, whilst two years later Michael Faraday experimented with the polarisation of light by magnetic fields. Each of these developments – and others – contributed to our understanding of the natural habitat. This understanding and knowledge has been of great benefit. Yet it is also possible to say that increased understanding has afforded the potential for mismanagement and corruption. It may not be long before 'designer babies' are widely available, and before star-wars laser weapons are available to the masses. The translation of energy between Uranus and Neptune, as occurs between 2003 and 2010, affords the perfect conditions for mankind to explore the particular genius that brings together science with imagination.

Even now, many people wonder if the unseen radiation linked to the use of mobile telecommunication devices might cause great damage to the delicate human biosystems of those who have come to rely on these devices. The incidence of associated cancers is likely to be high at the end of the decade. Those working to reduce the effect and, indeed, to cure those suffering from this action, may have difficulty in coping with the increased work-load created. Until the discontinuity of the translation of vibration between Uranus and Neptune ceases in 2010, many people may continue to ignore inherent risks.

We now know that Uranus, like Saturn has rings. To astrologers, these are powerful symbols suggesting that at some point restraint may be necessary. With Saturn, this restraint is usually applied through equal measures of feelings of inadequacy and fear: we become concerned that we might not act professionally enough or that in some way we will over-step the mark. Such concerns constrain those who might otherwise do damage to themselves and others. Uranus's rings are not quite as obvious. Whereas Saturn's rings can be viewed with a reasonably sophisticated telescope, Uranus's rings were unknown until the Voyager spaceship relayed its powerful images. Despite these symbols, mankind seems blissfully unaware that exciting advances bring with them difficulties that are unique and demanding.

It is usually at the point that Uranus moves from one sign to another that someone somewhere announces that enough is enough and questions the value of the gains supposedly made. Even so, until 2010 when the discontinuity outlined above becomes apparent, the intuitive technologies should continue to enjoy rapid development. The biotechnologies make significant progress too – though here, during the period that Pluto makes its path through Sagittarius (until 2008), questioning of the ethics could have a tempering effect. Long-term investment at the cutting edge of these industries may not seem so wise at the end of the decade, when the first claims against some of these products and services begin to have an impact. The share price of some of the companies involved could fall severely within months, as the suits come before the courts.

Of advantage to the short-term investor, however, may be growing interest by many individuals in community affiliations. The drive towards cooperative shopping movements looks set to gain pace. Before Uranus moves on into Aries, it may be that certain shops or goods are made available only to those who have declared a particular allegiance. This need not take an ethical dimension – though this is likely. It could even be the case that certain suppliers insist that their products are available solely to those who adhere to certain codes. Far-fetched as it may appear, the new 'iris recognition' systems could effectively bar some individuals from acquiring certain goods legally. While, on the one hand, this technology could assist parents in monitoring the foods eaten by their children away from home, that same technology could be used to impinge on liberty. The development of products providing new identification processes, together with products that affect their efficiency, and the service back-ups that these industries will spawn, may provide investment opportunities.

Uranus's entry into Aries in 2010 heralds a very different momentum. Replacing the visionary and intuitive features of the previous five years, a raw, demanding, forceful energy takes centre stage. The aesthetically pleasing innovation of previous years gives way to a more literal, cutting-edge technology – particularly between 2010 and 2013. We should anticipate the arrival of machines that use lasers or special metal technology and designs that are bold and geometric. There is a hard edge to Uranus's Aries transit. Those who tune in to the urgency of this transit will be difficult customers to please. They will want goods to be despatched immediately. This puts managers in a difficult position. It is possible that many of these 'cutting-edge' innovations will be made available before they are fully tried and tested. It would be wise for investors to exert caution. State-of-the-art goods may fail the test of time. It is probable that there will be a larger than normal number of business failures between 2010 and 2013 as young and inexperienced management teams discover they lack the resources and infrastructure to cater for an increasingly demanding clientele.

Aries is a sign often associated with military action. As alerted in an earlier chapter ('Water Wars'), the end of the decade promises to be a period of extreme tension. For companies to manage to deliver their products and services into areas at war will require courage and bravery. Those able to employ people who can meet these demands should enjoy a strong reputation and considerable profit.

The demand for military hardware at the end of the decade is likely to be high. Firms able to provide the required armaments should find a ready market for their products. Needless to say, this is likely to spawn demand for artificial limbs and other physical aids for those wounded in conflict. These will not be the only by-products of this period. The construction industry in most parts of the world will be affected also.

Uranus in Aries looks to fast, efficient, stream-lined office and living space. Driven, perhaps, by the need to supply affordable housing (and to re-house those displaced by war), there is likely to be increased demand for prefabricated homes. Firms able to provide energy-efficient, low-cost structures should experience fast growth over the eight-year period 2010–2018. Clearly, those firms supplying the materials for these 'pre-packed' initiatives will experience growth also.

Thanks to the information gleaned by the spaceship Voyager, we now know that Uranus spins on its axis in the opposite direction to all the other known planets of our solar system and that its magnetic poles are at variance with what might have been expected. These factors offer powerful suggestions of inherent instability. As Uranus makes its way through Aries – the first of the Fire signs of the zodiac – we might anticipate that some people will find the effect literally too hot to handle.

As outlined above, new items arriving in the marketplace will not have had time to be industry-tested. Flaws in these items, and the dangers created by mis-use, could give rise to accidents. In turn, those events could give rise to demands for other products and services. Most obviously, the requirements of the fire services will grow. Equally, those firms providing goods for the treatment of burns could find they are working extended hours to cope with demand.

Uranus's journey through the signs has links with developments in the world of broadcasting – the word itself encapsulating aired opinion designed to provoke discussion. When the planet last worked its way through Aries (1928–1934), one of the great technological breakthroughs was the transmission by the BBC of the first still pictures for television. Within a year the first full programmes were transmitted. A form of 'instant messaging' had arrived. It was during this period, too, that the first ship-to-shore telephone messages were received and sent. From those early days an entire industry has developed almost beyond recognition. It is hard to see what the next stage here can be: the teleportation of people? Is it possible that the 'beam-me-up' science-fiction associated with Star Trek will become reality? Perhaps the first advances here will take place between 2010 and 2018 as Uranus moves through the Aries sector.

The fast transportation of people from one place to another could be achieved in other ways too. In 1930 (when Uranus last moved through Aries), Sir Frank Whittle commenced his experiments with gas turbines for jet propulsion. Elsewhere, the first non-stop flight from Paris to New York was made. Travel to the opposite side of the globe without a stop-over, after 2010, seems a wholly acceptable forecast on the basis of those earlier achievements. Clearly, those who have invested in developing the essential fuels to enable this will find themselves on the crest of a new wave in transportation and associated industries.

Streamlining in the metal industries is probable too. In 1934, as Uranus was leaving the Aries section of the zodiac, the British iron and steel industries were reorganised, thus eliminating wasteful competition. A similar attitude to metal enterprises is likely as Uranus moves on into Taurus in 2015. Investors may find it worthwhile keeping their ear to the ground for discussions about these plans after 2008 – just a little before Uranus crosses *into* the Aries sector.

It is worth mentioning that when the planet last made its way through Aries there was a burgeoning understanding of the make-up of atoms, with much smaller particles within each atom being identified. This was the period when the meson was discovered. Scientists found it nearly impossible to identify exactly where these particles were since they moved so fast, and in so many directions. They embodied the principles of inherent unpredictability: a Uranus discovery indeed. Further sub-division of these particles could throw even more light on the nature of the universe and, in turn, yield extraordinary breakthroughs in medicine and travel.

In terms of travel, it appears that each time Uranus changes sign, the speed at which people can travel from one place to the next increases. As the planet makes its way though each sign of the zodiac, there is potential for the ordinary person to make full use of the breakthroughs made during the planet's passage through the earlier signs. There are clear links with the types of fuel used. We may well imagine that developments in the volatility of fuel (as with jet propulsion) will pave the way for the faster transcontinental voyages mentioned above.

Uranus passes from Aries into the Taurus sector of the zodiac in May 2018. Taurus is the first of the Earth signs. It is perhaps unsurprising that the world land-speed record was broken in 1936 when Uranus last journeyed through this sign. The standard car engine was modified to enable the vehicle to exceed previous speed targets. Sports cars of the period were not the only type of transport to benefit from this technical feat. Before long, what was taking place below the bonnet of the average saloon car owed much to those developments. We may anticipate similar developments as Uranus makes its way across the early degrees of Taurus in 2018. Indeed, a major distinguishing factor between the present time and 2020 is the further shrinking of the global village as people use new vehicles to travel quickly and easily between continents.

Activity in the Taurus zone of the tropical zodiac correlates with significant developments in world currencies. Uranus's arrival in this sign, together with the approaching Jupiter–Saturn conjunction, due to occur in 2020, could be indicative of significant developments in this area. It seems probable that the number of hard currencies available will change during this period. Whilst it may still be early days for the launch of a global currency, a move towards such an economic vehicle may be widely discussed.

12

Wall Street and London Markets, 2004–2020

Previous chapters have highlighted trends and difficulties to be faced in the coming years. This chapter analyses specific periods. Potentially important trading dates are alerted and discussed. As these times approach, and with the benefit of information of the time, it will be possible to identify more accurately the extent of volatility or price change to be expected. The years between 2004 and 2020 are defined within six sections: 2004–2005, 2005–2007, 2007–2009, 2009–2013, 2013–2018 and 2018 to 2020. Before looking at these periods, it is worth mentioning a special period that encompasses the years 2004 to 2012. These years may afford a particular opportunity for the discerning investor.

On 8 June 2004, the inhabitants of Europe, Africa (except western parts), the Middle East and most of Asia (except eastern parts) will witness one of the rarest of planetary alignments. Venus will eclipse the Sun.[1] The planet's transit across the solar disc will take the better part of four hours. This event will recur in June 2012 but will not then happen again until the year 2117. These very special eclipses occur in pairs separated by eight years, and always in either early June or early December. The most recent of these rare solar eclipses took place in 1874 and 1882 and were wildly celebrated events. The composer J. Philip Sousa was commissioned to write a march[2] for the occasion and the citizens of Washington were able to enjoy his music whilst witnessing the extraordinary spectacle in the sky above them.

The history of Art and Music shows these repeating eight-year pockets of time to coincide with prolific artistic activity: the period 1631–1639 found Rubens, Van Dyck, Rembrandt and Velazquez producing some of their finest work, whilst in music Monteverdi was making his indelible mark.[3] The next period, 1761–1769, saw another outpouring of artistic talent.[4] Mozart began his grand tour as a child in 1763. Meanwhile, Haydn was delivering his Great Mass with Organ. London in 1768 saw the foundation of the Royal Academy whose first President was to be the portrait painter, Joshua Reynolds. The most recent period, 1874–1882, witnessed a wide spectrum of artistic creativity through the talents of Cézanne, Manet, Monet, Renoir, Saint-Saëns, Bizet, Dvořák, Smetana, Sisley, Borodin, Degas, Delibes, Grieg, Brahms, Rodin and many others.[5]

Potentially, should the influence repeat, the world of Art, Theatre and Music will enjoy a renaissance in the coming years. Indeed, whilst many earlier artists had to wait years (even after their deaths in some cases) for recognition, there is a possibility that by 2020 some of the works created between 2004 and 2012 will be seen to have gained in value. Whilst the capital funding of these enterprises may cause concern to those directly involved, the demand for such works could increase in the coming decade and beyond. Indeed, it is possible that investment in arts between 2004 and 2012 could yield good returns for the long-term investor.

During this same period, it is possible that the leisure sectors of the Wall Street, Tokyo, London, Frankfurt and Paris Stock Exchanges will gain ground – despite some difficulties between 2005 and 2007. A growing or revived need to appreciate specific goods rather than gambles on equity price rises, would affect both artistic endeavours and areas of the commodity markets – most particularly precious metals and jewels. It is possible that we may see evidence of a rise in prices here during June and July 2004.

This makes sense from another perspective. Just prior to this extraordinary astronomical event, Venus appears to turn retrograde in the sky (astronomically, a prerequisite for the transit of Venus to take place). The position of the planet on the day when Venus appears to cease movement in the sky (17 May 2004) finds the planet exactly opposite the Galactic Centre – traditionally a marker for a fall in prices. This could be an interesting day in the global marketplace. What occurs around this time could well leave investors pondering their situation. Many may choose to abandon the equity markets in favour of commodities, creating increased demand in this area. By the time of the Venus transit itself, the price of commodities, particularly of gold and other precious metals and jewels, could have risen sharply. Venus is, after all, associated with all that brings pleasure.

For thousands of years, Venus has been affiliated with both copper and emeralds. A marked change in the respective values of these metals in particular seems likely. It is probable that copper will gain significantly in value over the coming eight years as it is discovered to have properties even greater than have previously been understood. With developments in the next generation of mobile phones, and in computers, perhaps requiring copper as a key component, the price of this metal might increase sharply during the 'Venusian period 2004–2012'.

The price of gold,[6] having passed the important $400 mark in the autumn of 2003, would seem likely to gather further pace during 2004. Other precious metals, most particularly those employed in nuclear processes, should also enjoy an increase in value. Those investors anticipating a rise in these commodities are unlikely to be disappointed as their portfolios outstrip those of other investors investing solely in equities. These developments are likely to capture the headlines and would doubtless appear as a welcome boost in an otherwise indifferent marketplace. Whereas, in the past, many individuals kept a weather eye on the FTSE or Dow Jones indices and were captivated by the wild fluctuations in their values, such drama may be found elsewhere – most probably in commodity indices.

The Transit of Venus is not, of course, the only astronomic or cosmic event that could influence trade and trading conditions in 2004. From the very last day of 2003, Uranus begins its geocentric, seven-year journey through the tropical zodiac sign of Pisces. Uranus's orbit of approximately 84 Earth years results in its stay in each sign being approximately 7 years. Its previous transit through this sign (1920–1927) witnessed great change on the world economic stage as new concepts and breakthroughs entered the commercial arena. In the USA especially, stock-market indices thrived.

Analysis of the markets of 1920 to 1927 shows particular types of stocks to have made fast gains. These were stocks associated with new technologies of the period. Radio and air travel were the innovative platforms of the day. Today's equivalent encompasses the media, telecommunications and biotechnics. The coming years should find considerable excitement in these investment areas. Even so, we ought perhaps to remember that it was at the end of that period that markets finally collapsed, in October 1929. Should the same pattern return, then investments in these sectors especially could come unstuck very early in the next decade.

History shows that in every set of quarterly stock-market figures, from 1922 to 1929 (roughly coinciding with Uranus' passage through Pisces), the Dow Jones industrial average was up on the year before.[7] There may have been many reasons for this. Certainly the spread of electrical power helped to increase productivity. Workers could earn more. Perhaps more important, however, was the relative easy with which people could gain credit, and with the burgeoning advertising industry alerting many to a variety of new products, the middle classes of the period gained experience of 'Buy now, Pay later'.

There are other parallels between the present and the 1920s. Then, the imagination of many investors was caught by Lindbergh's flight.[8] A boom in airline stocks followed, though it was many years before commercial airlines were in operation and bringing in revenue. Uranus is the planet associated with future technology – scientific advances that might be described as being at the cutting edge. The sign of Pisces covers intuitive talents. The two factors together suggest that fads and fancies will form an unusual alliance during this time. Already, through touch-screen televisions and even touch-technology clothing, there are signs of new markets opening. The imagination of many investors may be captured by present-day developments. Related stocks could boom.

That said, the transit of Uranus through Pisces from 2003 to 2011 is different from that of the 1920s. The present journey through Pisces is following hard on the heels of an exceedingly difficult trading period that began in 2000. Even venture capitalists are likely to remain shy of taking risks. Rapid growth in the value of equities appears unrealistic despite news of promising developments in biotechnologies, etc. The telecommunications industry will be particularly cautious about even the most exciting of new developments. This is unfortunate since there is evidence to suggest that breakthroughs already made could bring increased revenue to those investing in companies providing components for new hardware.

Analysis of the stock market prices of the 20th century shows that the passage of Saturn through the twelve zones of the tropical zodiac depresses the value of stocks associated with the zone or sign being transited. Until mid-2005, Saturn will be moving through the sign of Cancer. Cancer is the first of the Water signs of the zodiac. It is the sign associated with the home and with essential nourishment. Industry sectors associated with this sign include the construction industry, food production and security.

Saturn revisits this sign approximately every 30 years – its last stay in Cancer being 1974–1976. In the West and in those areas where property is seen as an investment, such periods tend to coincide with times of re-evaluation of property prices and deep concern about the same. The United Kingdom is not alone in experiencing this particular effect although it may be argued that it feels it more acutely than other nations. There appears to be a close correlation between Saturn's transit through a sign and enhancement of particular fear factors. During this planet's Cancer odyssey, concern over rising levels of debt, and uncertainty about interest rates, result in a

growing depressive atmosphere that finally pervades the banking community, which responds by reducing or even withdrawing support to those
whose survival depends on a more flexible attitude.

The anxiety levels of investors who left the market following the débâcle
of 2000 may very well increase under these conditions. Large numbers of
these individuals could delay their return to the markets – perhaps unknow-
ingly choosing to wait until Saturn leaves this sign in mid-2005.
Reluctance to engage in trading is a further indication of sluggish conditions in the general marketplace. Even so, Saturn will be moving away from
its opposition to the Galactic Centre – a position that brought severe market
torment in January and May 2003. This suggests that the depressed market
levels reached in these months will set the low benchmark for the
2003–2005 period. Those who stayed to weather these storms could find
their persistence rewarded as the indices begin to move forward.

Even so, both the USA and the UK could find 2004 a difficult year, with
marked growth most unlikely. Wall Street and London markets seem likely
to experience turbulence in May 2004 with aftershocks reverberating for
some weeks. Indeed, it may be late summer before recovery begins.
Difficulties faced by the exchequers of both countries suggest that decisions
will be taken to increase taxes – further depleting the resources of those who
might have been encouraged to return to the investment arena. As indicated in an earlier chapter, the USA will probably experience a particularly
difficult time in 2004. Undoubtedly this will affect American indices – and,
subsequently, those of other trading nations – making stress in the marketplace highly probable during the last few months of the year.

Stock market dramas have been a regular feature of the October and
November trading landscapes for many years. It is possible that this is in
part due to the Sun's passage through the sign of the scales (Libra), when
the focus turns to balance and harmony. Stocks that have been over-valued
tend to experience a downward trend at this time of year as markets attempt
to restore harmony and level-headedness. There are signs that 2004 may be
no exception. Clues as to what lies ahead may be apparent on 5 October.
This date is likely to prove a turning point in the commodity markets –
particularly with regard to gold, whose price moves could be marked.

On 13 October, there is a solar eclipse in the sign of Libra. Imbalance
in market activity is probable from this date with falls likely on both 19
and 22 October. Recovery should be apparent during the first week of
November. On 11 November 2004, Mars moves into the sign of Scorpio –
a feature that has been common to various stock market dramas in the past.

115

This is an interesting date in other respects. Uranus will appear stationary in the sky (as viewed from Earth) and will have travelled a fifth of its cycle in relation to Pluto. The drama this time could take the form of a sudden and marked up-swing when news of a scientific breakthrough is announced. Venus makes her Scorpio ingress on 22 November. This date marks the start of a week that might be described as 'regulating'. Falls are possible through to Wednesday (the 24th). A bounce back from this date is probable. By Tuesday, 30 November, as Mercury reaches the Galactic Degree – where it 'stations' – a peak is likely to be reached. We might then expect a pull back to 20 December when once again there is a turning point. This should result in 2004 ending on a bright note – though the dizzying heights of March 2000 are not to be seen for many years.

We have already mentioned the astrological charts of nations. The economic chart for the United Kingdom, still resonating today, is set at midnight, Westminster, 1 January 1801.[9] It was long noted that this Capricorn-based chart would be affected by Neptune's passage across the base of the chart from 1989 onward. The presence of Neptune, the planet associated with water and the sea, across this vulnerable area indicated potential difficulty associated with a shift in the UK's water-table, and subsequent susceptibility of various regions to flooding. This is now beyond dispute and already there is talk of some properties being uninsurable – thus damaging their value irrevocably. This flood factor alone would be enough to reduce property values. Coupled with Saturn's presence in Cancer and a potential slow-down in this market, the effect could be dramatic. Interest rates too may rise in the autumn of 2004. These combined forces could create misery for many property owners. Further, these factors could impact on the way in which people live. More and more individuals may choose to rent rather than carry the burden of property ownership.

From another perspective, should property values fall and large numbers of the population be unable to move house, ever greater effort may be made to improve the condition of those same properties. Thus, whilst Saturn's presence in Cancer looks to be bad for estate agents, it could be of benefit to the home-decorating industry and, perhaps, the building-work sector.

The sign of Cancer is associated with food and the nation's bread basket. People have to eat to survive. Even so, a chill wind may blow through the food industry and general household good sectors. Mention has been made of the 179-year solar, and subsequent weather, cycles.[10] It is clear that these forces are at work and that the effect of climate change on crops has been significant. During 2004 it is probable that the price of grain commodities will increase. This is likely to affect weekly housekeeping costs considerably. Rises here further support the idea that available funds for investment will be limited.

Analysis of the various blue chip companies of the FTSE 250 show many to have been incorporated while the Sun was moving through the sign of Cancer. One of the traits linked to Cancer is sustainability and good husbandry. It is hardly surprising that firms should stand the test of time when these traits form part of their underlying, and often unseen, astrological mission statement. Their commitment to long-term strategies is considerable. Further, many of these business have weathered Saturn's transits through Cancer in the past. They have experience and know which actions to avoid.

Many well-known brands could face difficulties during 2004. When Saturn made its way through Gemini, we saw depression hit both telecommunications and travel-related stocks. Those firms engaged in developing new products in either area were sustained only by the investment of visionaries, who believed that growth would come – in time. This time it is likely to be the turn of companies and firms seeking support for sustainable growth, and developing new food markets (including GM products), who will find the period to mid July 2005 extremely difficult. They too may have to depend for support on investors committed to particular causes. The more staid investors – pension fund managers and bankers – may be unwilling to support these developments, preferring instead to see evidence that research and development costs are being kept to a minimum.

Good husbandry also covers personal banking. The winds blowing here may be more than chill. Between June 2003 and July 2005, it could feel as though Siberian winters have arrived. In the UK, this will affect not just the big four banks, but also many building societies. Of course, the fall in their popularity would be linked with the rising number of people forced into negative equity. However, this factor alone is not sufficient to justify the backlash that this group of businesses will experience. The trend towards Internet banking looks set to continue. Many bank branches will close as more people find a different way of moving their money around.

Forecasting trends in any period warrants more than a cursory look at the passage of one planet through a particular sign, however. Saturn's transits provide an interesting backdrop but they are not the only factor at work. The journeys of the other planets through the various tropical zodiac sectors offer further information. Analysis of these suggests that the sectors most likely to experience growth between 2003 and September 2004 will be related to the service-industry. Of the very many types of companies that fall into this category there are: laundry services, database management services, office-cleaning, DIY products, packaging suppliers, storage providers, local bus services, delivery agents and, as always, skilled craftsmen.

Whilst companies providing these products and services can look forward to growth in demand through this period, managers might like to bear in mind that this same period could see a rise in the activity of unions and trade associations. Strikes – or at least the threat of strikes – are likely, with subsequent disruption to services and distribution. Obviously it would be necessary to assess each particular company or industry to be more specific as to the probability and times of potential stress.

During this period (to mid-2005), investors who have fallen foul of the stock market may well choose to invest in local craftsmen and to lend their expertise to co-operative ventures. Investing in small factory outlets might well produce rapid gains. Curiously, whilst it has been the norm to allow a new company two years before it begins to return a profit, this is unlikely to be needed for craftsmen in 2004. Their value is likely to soar and funding their business development could prove a profitable route for many.

Let us return now to the Venus transit mentioned at the start of this chapter. Venus is linked to two signs, Taurus and Libra. On 25 September 2004, Jupiter will move into the latter sign – within days of the Sun beginning its annual transit of Libra. A sudden burgeoning in the demand for leisure products and high fashion is likely. Many firms could be seduced into spending more on marketing than they can really afford during the autumn of 2004. Investors may wish to keep a wary eye on escalating costs here. (But those whose portfolios include investment in advertising companies could gain.)

Jupiter's tour of the zodiac takes just under twelve years. During its transit of Libra, there is greater than usual interest in marriages between companies. These do not necessarily take the form of take-overs. It is rather more common to find that companies see ways of effecting mergers that benefit both parties. The last few days of September 2004 should see this type of business news announced on the front pages of newspapers. Share prices would obviously be affected. Since there may be little written warning that these events are to take place, investors might like to be aware of the possibilities from late March 2004 and to keep a weather eye on company news from that date. Of specific interest here would be telecommunications companies and firms providing components for IT products.

Finally, it is possible to use the study of planet cycles to identify specific groups of people who have much to offer the business community. Most specifically, companies employing individuals born during two very special periods are at an advantage. The early days of April 1975 and the latter days of September 1976 witnessed the birth of two extraordinarily creative groups of people. Of these, those working in the fields listed above could find their talents coming to the fore: 2004 may well prove to be one of their finer years and greatly benefit the companies with whom they are involved.

2005–2007 |

The extraordinarily high level of activity on the sun, as illustrated by the number of visible sunspots in the year 2000, should subside in the coming years and minima reached around 2008. The intervening years ought to see a marked reduction in sunspot numbers until that low level is reached. As the number of sunspots decreases, history shows that investors have a tendency to retrench and to take fewer risks. The effect this has on market activity can be to reduce the volume of trade. This does not necessarily mean a decrease in values, but in the years 2005 to 2007 it indicates a change in attitude reflected in a conservative, if any, increase in market values. There may be other indicators of change in investing trends.

A trailing off in interest in both day and peripheral trading may be apparent following the lunar eclipse of 24 April 2005. This eclipse lies across the Taurus/Scorpio axis of the zodiac. Whilst it would be quite wrong to suggest that every time the sign of Scorpio is involved there are market falls, it does seem true that there is greater likelihood of turbulent and negative action during these periods. In this particular case, Chiron, the planetoid that would appear to have some association with accountability, will take up a prominent position over both Wall Street and London – both markets could be affected by an accounting or auditing scandal that is most uncomfortable for traders. This could prove the last straw for some.

In an earlier chapter it was also shown that, should history repeat itself, the USA could experience economic pressures in 2004. As was shown above, Wall Street may be spared a negative end to 2004 by advances in both biotechnology and telecommunication companies. Even so, it seems probable that advances made will be halted in the last few weeks of March 2005.

Underlying concerns about former blue chip companies no longer being able to deliver the dividends of the past could depress many investors. This could prove a major factor in depressing both London and Wall Street markets in the week beginning 21 March 2005. A general lowering of profit/earnings ratios – specifically in older companies – would also ring alarm bells for some fund managers. Some may turn their attention back to the commodity markets before the end of that month. Activity here could peak on 28/29 March. Perhaps the most difficult date for both markets will be 24 April, however, when the above-mentioned lunar eclipse coincides with an important phase in Mars's cycle relative to Earth.

Towards the end of June 2005, from both the heliocentric and geocentric perspectives, Saturn makes its move into the Leo zone of the tropical zodiac. Should Saturn apply the brakes to industries and companies associated with this sign, as it has depressed associated sectors when it has passed through other signs, then a downturn in stocks linked to the leisure industries is probable. Companies involved in this sector may issue profit-warnings for this period.

In the opening paragraphs of this chapter it was explained that the Venus transit of 2004 marks the start of an eight-year period of potentially prolific artistic activity. The real surge in creative expression is likely to come as the sunspots increase in number after the expected minima in 2008. Whilst leisure industry stocks could suffer generally as Saturn makes its way through Leo, a surge of creativity and prolific output may be apparent in the work of artists of this period. Artists seeking funding may be quick to remind potential sponsors of the gains that can be made when their project captures the public's imagination. Seductive as the idea of acting as a theatrical 'angel' may be for some, it seems most unlikely that rewards will be plentiful for some years. Shows launched during this period may be short-lived. The exception to this rule being shows that have proved to stand the test of time. The classics could win through in 2005 and 2006.

Perhaps because the general public is more receptive to the idea of reducing debt, or simply because global conditions are such that spending on leisure activity seems inappropriate, growth in leisure-related stocks will probably slow down markedly from June 2005. Even ticket sales for movies could slump between 2005 and 2007. Against this backdrop it might appear surprising that precious metals and jewels will at least hold, if not increase, their value throughout 2005 and 2006. This, though, would be an apt expression of the need to own something that brings pleasure but which also provides security.

One interesting feature of 2005 is that the early months of the year could find governments on both sides of the Atlantic Ocean focused on gaining extra revenue from gambling and associated industries. By early July 2005, discussions about limiting or taxing such gains could gather momentum. It will be interesting to see which associated laws are passed in the early days of July 2005. The cost of policing these laws promises to be far greater than expected and may not offer either government the passport to extra revenue that they assumed they had identified. This same period may see a surge in the number of gambling enterprise companies based off-shore.

Indeed, many governments, particularly those in the West, faced with a growing number of companies using the Internet to sell products and services and using off-shore facilities to host their domains, may express concern as to how to maintain revenue. Throughout 2005 and 2006, the governments of some countries may conclude that there is merit in at least debating the value of creating an international tax-collecting facility.

One interesting sector to watch for growth from late October 2005 is financial services. Having weathered the storms of the last few years and regained some confidence through better-policed accounting coupled with greater general understanding of the role these experts play, many people could feel more inclined to use these professional services. Insurance companies too should enjoy a rather better press and subsequently increased business between autumn 2005 and 2006. This particular twelve-month period could witness bumper gains in this sector.

The autumn of 2005 does not appear to offer the bumpy investment ride that has occurred in some years. Indeed, though there are indicators that between 14 and 22 November 2005 some sectors could experience a change in share direction, investors may be cautiously optimistic that the global trend is towards growth. Even so, investors in the banking and insurance sectors might consider taking profits *before* September 2006, when the financial climate is scheduled for further change.

Six months prior to this, there is a total eclipse of the Sun on 29 March 2006. The path of this eclipse gives visibility to those in the northern tip of Brazil, Atlantic Ocean travellers, the people of the northern regions of the African continent, the Black Sea, and those inhabiting the northern regions of Mongolia. This astronomically theatrical event will be much heralded since it may be viewed by a large proportion of the Earth's population. Rather less attention may be given to the fact that on that same day, Pluto will appear 'stationary' (i.e. stand still) in the sky close to the point considered to be the Galactic Centre.

It is most emphatically not true that markets suffer every time there is a total eclipse of the Sun. Even so, there is often a marked effect on people's behaviour. This eclipse, in the tropical zodiac sign of Aries, may be accompanied by concern by some investors that certain economies are over-heating once more. The eclipse itself could trigger some drama.

Sadly, historical analysis of the possible correlation of dramatic market movement with Pluto's crossing of the Galactic Centre cannot be made. The last time Pluto made this crossing was in 1759 to 1760. This synchronised with Halley's comet's[11] regular return to the solar system and it is impossible, therefore, to say which of the two cosmic events had the greater influence. The stock markets of that period were very different from those in existence now. There is evidence that an early FTSE-type index in the United Kingdom fell throughout the months when Pluto passed over this point. However, there was nothing hugely dramatic about this – although it is possible that there might be a similar effect in 2006.

Far more significant was Lawrence Child's printing of the first banker's note[12] – a development that has affected the financial world ever since. The point about a bank note is that it implicitly demands a level of trust on the part of all those involved in the system. This is entirely in keeping with the symbolism of Pluto (a 'God of Wealth') crossing the Galactic Centre (and therefore affecting large numbers of people). It is entirely possible that Pluto's crossing of this point in 2006 will witness the advent of yet another form of currency, designed, this time, to be incorruptible and of value across the global economy.

There was one other interesting event that coincided with Pluto's journey through the latter degrees of Sagittarius. In France, one of the great trading nations of the world in 1760, the word 'silhouette' passed into French vocabulary as a derisory term meaning 'a figure reduced to its simplest form'. Etienne de Silhoutte[13] held the position of controller-general. He attempted reforms that included land taxes, a reduction in pensions and the melting down of silver for use as money. There were serious consequences for the French and for the countries with whom they traded. Indeed, within a year the global trading picture had changed. It is to be anticipated that Pluto's crossing of the Galactic Centre in 2006 could coincide with a variation of this drama, with a similar global impact. Here, an educated guess is possible. It seems reasonable to suppose that January 2006 will witness a shift of emphasis and the dawn of a new financial era. Might this be the time when a well-known currency gives way to the Euro or US dollar? One option would be for sterling to give way to the Euro. Clearly this would significantly affect the global economic picture.

Neptune and Pluto form an interesting alignment on 29 January 2006 – just as they did between 11 October 1967 and August 1968. The latter ten-month period was a time of extraordinary activity on the global financial stage. On 18 November 1967 the British Pound was devalued.[14] Meanwhile, the price of gold was on the move. The United States, together with six Western European nations, determined to sell no more gold to private buyers.[15] The First Philadelphia Bank installed a cash dispenser,[16] thus making an early move towards automated banking. Meanwhile, BankAmericard holders[17] increased dramatically in number. Growth in demand for these cards would soon result in the birth of Mastercard and other credit card facilities. In the space of a few short months, the financial world changed.

As outlined above, the period around the solar eclipse of late March 2006 and the ensuing six weeks suggests a degree of volatility. Thereafter, however, it appears probable that indices generally will rise – at least until late August 2006. We could conclude that the UK will take the decision to abandon Sterling in favour of the Euro during the early months of 2006 and that this would be a contributory factor to some turbulence. By mid-May any volatility could subside and indices generally could enjoy an upward turn for some months.

The closing months of 2006 do not appear quite as positive as those of the middle of the year. As the 'Water Wars' chapter explains, a slow build of planetary tension suggests that the last years of this first decade will be difficult. It could be argued that this tension begins in the autumn of 2006. The political landscape of this period looks interesting. Socialism in a variety of forms may be on the increase. Analysis of the Saturn–Neptune synodic cycle during the 20th century clearly shows that each time these two planets have come to critical phases in their cycle, increased interest in this ideology becomes apparent. Unless this pattern is broken, then we should anticipate a marked swing to the political left in the later months of 2006. Several stock markets could react to this development by turning downward. In keeping with the autumns of so many years past, it seems probable that a downturn will be evident – most particularly in the last few days of October.

There are also signs of negative thinking in stock markets in the first weeks of 2007, but by early March of that year the atmosphere changes, and once again there could be signs of recovery. Significantly perhaps, travel and telecommunication stocks that suffered so badly in the opening years of the decade could enjoy growth. This revival, and a consequent acceleration in various indices, will no doubt be of great comfort to those whose financial positions were precarious just a few years before.

To a greater or lesser degree we are all affected by the lunar phases. It may be that we are equally affected by the Moon's proximity to us. On 17 April 2007, the Moon will arrive at her closest point to Earth for some centuries, causing the neap or spring tides to reach new heights. The reaction of those working in the markets could also be exceptional. Indeed, the two-week period until the Full Moon on 2 May could see significant activity on the world's markets, with extremes reached throughout this period. Given that Manhattan Island is surrounded on three sides by water (which is most definitely influenced by the Moon), reactions on Wall Street could be momentous. Indeed, it could take some weeks for the situation to calm. Significantly, several planets appear to be moving in retrograde motion during the summer months of 2007. This implies a steadying force at work. There are political repercussions. During these months, resurgence in traditionally left-wing or even communist thinking takes hold. Elections held during this period should see a swing in that direction.

These swings from one position to the next could, in part, be due to the waning influence of the Moon as it pulls back from its proximity to Earth. By September, equity prices are on the move once more with a determination by some to see advances in particular sectors – most notably all those that are deemed to be particularly innovative.

September 2007–November 2008

This period promises to be one of the most challenging of the coming twenty years – and not solely in terms of global stock-market behaviour. The planetary alignment for this period is awesome. There are times when four planets stand at right-angles to one another – as if each is pulling in a different direction. Obviously, any one of these planets is at a critical stage in its synodic cycle with the other planet. To have so many cycles reach critical points simultaneously suggests tension of a very high degree.

Three other factors should be considered too. First, this period is likely to mark a sunspot minimum. Again, as we saw earlier, such moments in the solar cycle often prove to be turning points in social and economic, if not political, affairs. Secondly, the square formation marked by the planets is positioned around the Cardinal points of the zodiac. These points mark the solstice and equinoctal points – the moments when the seasons change in response to the Sun's position. Thirdly, the Moon will be travelling closer to Earth than has been the case for some time. The Moon's pull on water is well documented. It is worth reminding ourselves that the human body has a high water content and that each of us will feel this energy shift. Our responses will vary, though it seems fair to suggest that the responses of market-traders and investors could result in a high level of volatility in commercial dealing.

Clearly, if one planet is in the early degrees of a sign and that planet is part of a formation that sees three other planets at right-angles to one another, then those planets too must be making their entry into a new sign. These ingress points are always of interest as they correlate with shifts of attitudes and sensitivities.

Pluto makes its geocentric Capricorn ingress on 26 January 2008. This sector of the zodiac is associated with the activities of large institutions and corporations. Those who are tuned to Pluto's vibration become alert to the value of change through the elimination of waste, and through other forms of profound upheaval – including the need to face the 'death' of parts that may not achieve fruitfulness for much longer. In the world of commerce, the down-sizing of corporations is likely to become the norm once Pluto becomes firmly established in this sign.

This type of activity may not be driven by purely financial considerations. Change in the political landscape could leave some Chief Executives facing difficult dilemmas. A major factor might be changes in taxation – perhaps including large penalties for unacceptable waste emissions. Another possibility is that new rules giving more rights to workers and guaranteeing levels of pensions will create major disquiet in boardrooms across the world. The effect of down-sizing by companies thought to be secure would no doubt depress equities.

In the space of a few short years, global institutions and brand-names will doubtless disappear to be replaced by very different, smaller entities most likely to be family-controlled. It is interesting to note that when Pluto passed through Capricorn in the 18th century, rising concern about the quality of life of the citizens led politicians of the day to promote the *concept* of pensions. Concern about the *level* of pensions and social-fund care could head many agendas this time around. The difference now may be that families determine that they are better placed to look after their collective needs than political states have been.

It is in May 2009 that Jupiter, Chiron and Neptune appear as one in the sky. Conjunctions (where two planets appear to share the same zodiacal longitude), have traditionally been seen as seed moments. New ideas or products come to centre stage and their development may then be traced throughout the ensuing cycle. This extraordinarily rare 'triple' conjunction, when applied to attitudes to finance, suggests the dawn of a co-operative and egalitarian approach. Should global corporations begin to disband, two possibilities may be identified. The first would be the transfer of the wealth and power of these institutions to local employees – and perhaps to their families. The other option is that governments may take over the running of some enterprises, even if only temporarily.

However, just as large companies are likely to come apart at the seams as Pluto makes its way through Capricorn, so too may governments. Indeed, it is not hard to imagine that the rare triple conjunction mentioned above, which occurs in the high-tech sign of Aquarius, could see professional politicians who speak on behalf of thousands, replaced by voting systems that allow every citizen to have his or her say. The year 2009 marks the dawn of a new and exciting political age.

Yet another possibility is that governments at odds with one another will put pressure on each other's corporations, denying these the ability to trade as they had been doing. The strength and wealth of these institutions may then be passed to the nation or, perhaps, to the employees.

Talk of war is not necessarily bad news for stock markets. Indeed, even within the opening years of conflict, share prices have been seen to rise: 1915 is marked as one of the best years for equities[18] in the 20th century. It seems astounding that this should have been the case, just one year into the global war of the period. The United States has an impressive track record in this respect. During this early period, US President Woodrow Wilson, having given permission for war-related trade,[19] thus ensured his country would do brisk business and that equity markets would benefit as a result. It is not inconceivable that this situation could recur.

Quantifying the trade associated with war is not easy. Governments and their agents are naturally reluctant to let others know their position. The amount of ammunition or warheads held by each side in a dispute is for those involved in the war itself to know, and for others to guess. Those 'others' may well be investors, keen to assume that 'their companies' are providing those essential goods and services. The stock of such firms inevitably rises – even when facts about them are few, and hard to come by.

Stock markets around the world, then, should find this to be a period of growth despite global tension. Indeed, from the beginning of the second quarter of 2008, equity growth could go unchecked for more than a year.

Early signs that all is not what it seems may become apparent over a year later, in mid September 2009. Lack of controls, accidents and industrial unrest could give clues to possible difficulties. Once again, newspaper head-lines focus on the October effect, which on this occasion may be rather more apparent in early November. Then, the haunting themes of the calamities of the opening years of the decade are heard once more. Lay-offs and down-sizing become the buzz-words of the day and a reversal of stock-market gains begins in earnest. Venus's Scorpio ingress on 9 November marks the start of a down wave that does not recover until around 21 November. This first fall on Wall Street is followed by another in mid December, when Mars appears to stand still in the sky, prior to appearing to travel in retrograde motion for some weeks. This latter effect could mark a downturn that does not recover until the beginning of the following year.

A lunar eclipse on the last day of December 2009 marks the beginning of a tense fortnight through to the solar eclipse of 15 January 2010. This lunar eclipse further underlines the probability that mankind will greet the New Year (2010) with considerable apprehension.

Wall Street, 2009–2013 |

In his book *Sun – Earth – Man*, Theodor Landscheit highlighted the years 2002–2011 as a period of major instability.[20] Based on the relationship between Jupiter and the Centre of Mass of the solar system, his account showed how such periods in the past had coincided with years of extraor-dinary change. The most recent of these took place between 1968 and 1972. Few would disagree that this was a period of upheaval and rebellion in many parts of the world (China's Cultural Revolution and the war in Vietnam). It was also a time of excitement, when the future beyond known boundaries attracted much attention. Achievements in space travel and shifts in perspective effected significant cultural change. Global economics too were changed by the world events that occurred during this period. Narrowing Landscheit's time-frame by incorporating planet-configuration tensions at the end of the decade, the years 2009 to 2013, suggests that events which take place then will be long remembered, as are those of 40 years earlier.

Indeed, in the 'Water Wars' chapter we saw how the planetary shapes at the end of this first decade of the 21st century could coincide with man-made catastrophe on Earth. History provides telling examples as to how nations reacted to similar planetary tension in the past. If, as seems to be the case, the movements of the planets bring about certain reactions on Earth, then the global stock markets of these years also promise to be particularly challenging. At worst, financial meltdown could occur if the credit bubble bursts. At best, we may be propelled into a new age of financial management.

It is unfortunate that we cannot look back to similar alignments in the past to see what, if any, economic changes took place. Global stock markets simply did not exist hundreds of years ago when some of these planetary formations last occurred. It is true that the commodities markets of Europe over the last seven hundred years are fairly well documented and that some inference can be drawn through analysis of movements in these prices. However, there are too many differences between those earlier periods and present-day activity to enable easy delineation of the financial future. Even so, understanding the principles at work yields interesting clues, and following these threads of thought makes it possible to draw conclusions.

Considerable cosmic tension is forecast for November 2009. While it is not possible to state for certain that the sunspot minima will have been reached, as the solar cycle can be unpredictable, it is nevertheless probable. We can, though, be certain that various planet cycles will reach a critical phase. It is of particular interest that on 9 November 2009 Saturn will lie at right-angles to Pluto, with both journeying through the early degrees of the all-important Cardinal signs. It is most unlikely that this alignment will pass without notice. Indeed, at the very least, it is around this date that we may hear news of the decision to break up a large conglomerate. This event alone could be enough to send investors running for cover. Another possibility is that there will be a major pensions scandal connected to a global corporation. The knock-on effect of this could be financially catastrophic for many. Equally disquieting may be news that several governments are taking up positions that many view as intransigent. A curb, or even a drop, in market activity between 9 and 21 November is possible as despondent and negative thinking takes hold.

Even so, some market recovery is probable during the early part of the following month. It is at this time that Jupiter makes conjunctions first with Chiron and then with Neptune. Both events should be seen as moments when new ideas are thrown into the melting pot. As Jupiter is involved, it is probable that the world at large will hear of these adventures – and that some people, craving signs of an upturn, will rejoice at breakthroughs made, and be willing to invest. Should it be that these breakthroughs are linked with faster travel – and even, perhaps, to unknown areas of space – the anticipation of brave new worlds opening up may be palpable. Share prices in associated companies could move quickly over a few weeks. Again, in the last few weeks of 2009 there is likely to be news of advances linked to alternative medical practices. Another area ripe for take-off concerns fast-moving developments in the transmission of information. News from these various fronts will excite some and offer investors new markets that promise to grow quickly.

Away from the marketplace, many individuals could respond to these planetary themes by taking part in peace protests. Averting conflict (or further conflict) will be of far greater concern to the majority than market speculation. Sadly, the vested interests of some people may not be thwarted, and rising prices could be halted quickly as events on the global political stage take a dramatic turn in the run up to the lunar eclipse of 31 December. Escalation in hostilities is then probable and war may appear inevitable. Even if it does not, a generally negative mood could take hold early in 2010 – at least until Mars appears to stand still in the sky on 10 March. This date should prove to be a turning point.

Throughout 2010 there are implications that the smooth running of trading operations will not be possible. The potential for disruption of services – probably due to military or even terrorist activity – is greatest towards the end of June and throughout the early days of July. Trading in the more traditional sense could be problematic in the extreme. Those skilled in crisis-management techniques should find a ready market for their services during the summer of 2010.

Whilst daily stock-exchange activity could be disrupted over these dates, tension is likely to continue throughout July and August 2010. Chief Executives should take note of this. They may find that they are recalled from holiday if they risk being away from their desks at this critical time. It would be unwise for them to plan to be away for long during these months. Events are likely to change at a bewildering pace. Leadership skills will be needed at the various 'mission controls' of the banking world. Working from a distance may not be at all viable.

Again, the signs are that 'down-sizing' will be the key word. Those banks – and firms – that have not yet taken the decision to pare down their operations could take these steps as August 2010 draws to a close. The few firms able to expand their operations are most likely to be involved in armament production. This would no doubt pose awkward ethical questions for both private investors and fund managers. In the case of the former, many may find it preferable to be part of the growth-plan of smaller, local companies providing basic, non-military services, rather than maintain involve-ment with conglomerates struggling to cope during this difficult period – particularly given that these organisations may have links to the arms industries.

Needless to say, fund managers will no doubt find this period extraor-dinarily stressful. Identifying which companies are least vulnerable to prevailing forces, and making contact with those likely to flourish in a chaotic environment, will not be easy. It may be helpful for fund managers to look carefully at those companies whose top management personnel were born during that critical period in the mid-1960s when the Uranus–Pluto cycle began. This group of individuals has been identified elsewhere in this book. The planet combination under which they were born last occurred around 3000 BC. They think quite differently from their parents, grand-parents and even great-great-great-grandparents and beyond. Their perspective is unique. It is conceivable that their contribution at this time of stress will be extraordinary. The search to find individuals with imagi-nation, determination and a willingness to think along egalitarian and humanitarian lines should prove challenging for the head-hunters of this period. It will be those who fall into this category who should be the ideal leaders of the new business world that arrives when the critical moments are passed. Indeed, investing in firms able to find this expertise could prove one of the best moves ever for investors.

The middle months of 2010 may not be easy to negotiate. Pressure is all around and some may wonder if the human race can survive the period at all. Danger signals are everywhere. The solar eclipse of 11 July is heralded by a lunar eclipse in the banking sign of Capricorn just two weeks earlier on 26 June 2010. Around this time, disruption to world trade is likely, with the banks of some nations as exposed as some of their corporate counter-parts. The financial fault lines exposed during these months threaten to topple even some of the more apparently secure institutions.

This offers an opportunity for some. Merchant banks and so called 'friendly' or co-operative banking establishments, freed from political restraints, could find this period profitable. Of these institutions, those able to make fast decisions without recourse to other authorities should find they are able to access profit. Once again, these may be identified by careful study of the character of the individuals at the top. Those who are just a little maverick, with clear energy and vision, and a willingness to do business differently, are well placed to make the most of the opportunities that occur. By contrast, the national banks of China, Japan, the USA, the UK,

Australia, Canada and many other countries, should they respond to these planet chords, could experience a very difficult period indeed. There is ample reason to suggest that these institutions will be affected and that changes in their top management will occur as a direct result of inability by some to cope with the economic and political pressures of the period.

Those who weather the storms of July and August should be braced for obstacles of a different nature that threaten to buffet the markets in September. Mars's Scorpio odyssey (a period that recurs approximately every two years) usually marks significant movement in the marketplace. On 22 September 2010 (significantly this date is very close to the equinox and therefore to a natural shift both in the seasons and in man's reactions to events), Mars, in this sign, will lie at right-angles to Neptune (from the heliocentric perspective). This event should be seen as an alarm bell for investors. Global markets may be about to take yet another serious slither.

From the geocentric perspective, Mars will meet with Venus in Scorpio early in October – yet another factor that signals a potential fall in equity prices. On this occasion, Mars's presence in this sign and the cosmic dance these two planets play during the autumn months imply conditions that are best addressed by experts. Private investors may be well-advised to stay out of the global trading area throughout this period. One possibility is that commodity prices will rise quickly, only to fall before the year end. This turnaround in fortunes could be devastating for those unprepared for such volatility. Futures trading is likely to be aggressive and most certainly not for the faint-hearted.

The mood will shift dramatically in 2011 as the larger planets begin to pull away from one another, with many people experiencing glimpses of a future based on greater understanding and respect between nations. Thus 2011 promises to be singularly interesting. Where 2010 will be anticipated with dread by many, those same individuals will feel there is room for cautious optimism in the opening weeks of the following year. Of most particular interest is that there are no fewer than four solar eclipses in 2011. Not since the year 2000 will this number of eclipses have taken place in one year. Eclipses have long been seen as magical. They mark both endings and beginnings. Those years in which more than the normal two have taken place have proved to be years of particular historic interest. In the 20th century, few years featured four or more solar eclipses. These were 1917, 1935, 1946, 1964 and 1982. Within each of these years there were marked and accelerated shifts in social thinking; 2011 promises similar levels of change.

The first eclipse, on 4 January, and a subsequent one on 1 July, accentuate the eclipse axis of the previous year. Difficulties could continue. From the economic perspective both banking and blue-chip industries are likely to remain in turmoil. The two other eclipses of 2011 feature the Gemini – Sagittarius axis. This is vaguely reminiscent of the tortuous problems that beset the travel and telecommunications industries in 2002 and 2003 when this axis was similarly affected. This makes sense. If certain areas of the world are still involved in major warfare, pressure in these sectors would be understandable.

The planetary tension of the previous year looks likely to last until the last of the Jupiter–Saturn oppositions on 28 March 2011 (geocentric). This event normally marks a turning point in the general business cycle. It may be that the first quarter of the year sees the conclusion to military stress and strain.

Jupiter's move into Taurus (geocentric) on 4 June amplifies a return to constructive activity. By the time of its heliocentric ingress into that sign (September), this should be evident to all – most obviously demonstrated by activity in the construction industry. This, however, will not be the only industry sector to benefit. Taurus is, arguably, the sign most associated with 'wine, women and song'. There is appreciation of all the good things the Earth and its inhabitants can provide. If there has been a war, and it is in its concluding stages, then it would make sense for there to be growth in leisure activities that may have been curtailed over the previous years.

Again, if faith in banking has diminished (as seems likely), focus on a different kind of husbandry is probable. This would coincide with a sharp increase in the price of gold, already indicated for other reasons. Land and farming should also gain popularity. Whether because individuals feel they need simply 'to have a place of their own' or because there is a clear advantage in owning basic commodities, land values should increase.

Effects associated with an eclipse are as likely to be felt weeks and even months ahead of the event, as they are to be felt later. The connection between an event and an eclipse is identified through the sign in which the eclipse takes place, the angles between the planets at the time of the eclipse and the keywords associated with the zodiac signs accented. In the case of the last eclipse of 2011 (26 November), it is probable that change will have been observed in many regions of the world. This eclipse is partial, yet viewable from Cape Town to Melbourne. In both South Africa and Australia particularly, signs of economic advancement may be seen in the rising value of their respective indices from October onward. A beautiful equilateral triangle formed between Jupiter, Mars and Pluto, combined with the effects of this solar eclipse, suggests a move towards growth and prosperity. A cautionary note should be applied, however: these particular triangular patterns have been shown to have remarkable effects. Radio transmission is affected. Downturns in the marketplace have also been noted. But neither situation lasts for long. During the period when the aspect is exact (a day or so in this instance), despite apparent difficulties on the surface (daily index readings), good commercial progress can be made. Within a very short time, then, it should be possible to see considerable improvement – in this instance, most significantly in South Africa and Australia.

Positive developments may be seen in other areas also. The ingress of both Chiron and Neptune into Pisces in 2011 plays a crucial role as the second decade of the new millennium gets underway. The last time these two bodies passed through the sign of Pisces together was in the 1520s, when Neptune passed into Pisces in 1520 and Chiron followed in 1524. Given that the movements of both these celestial bodies offer a curious correlation with events in the history of medicine, it is not surprising that this period witnessed the breakthroughs made by the Swiss physician Paracelsus.[21] The impact his work has had on medicine has been considerable. Is it possible that a new 'Paracelsus' will emerge in 2011?

Most recently, Chiron visited Pisces in 1960, whilst Neptune last visited that sign in 1848. In both instances there were significant developments in the field of medicine. Crick and Brenner's[22] early work on DNA took a significant step forward in 1960. In 1848, as Neptune ventured into Pisces, early anaesthetic procedures began enabling huge strides in medicine.

It is reasonable, then, to suppose that there will be significant advances in the field of medicine in 2011 – though it is probable that not all will be free of difficulties. (During the 1960s the drug thalidomide was widely used, with devastating consequences for some.) It is to be hoped that gains will outweigh any disadvantages in the discoveries that lie ahead. Those who invest in this fast-growing sector could indeed reap extra rewards. Of particular interest might be a burgeoning number of sanctuaries and pre-operative centres that focus on getting the individual into peak condition *before* surgery is undertaken.

It is likely too that advances in drugs that improve mental health, coupled with awareness by some of the need to improve spiritual well-being, will introduce yet another approach to health management. Thus, it is not just physical health that is of particular fascination from 2011. Until 2018 especially, a focus on improving spiritual well-being gathers momentum. This is unlikely to be related to developments in religion. Much may be said and written about 'higher vibrations' during this period. Two themes could gain prominence here. The first is a resurgence in the Greek idea of music as a mode of abstract thought. This could give rise to singular developments in artistic activity. Music has an expressive power beyond what we hear. Study of higher, inaudible frequencies has shown that when these are present, humans may experience the 'paranormal'. These peculiar frequencies and the power they unleash could also gain authority over these years.

There may be few people working in this field during the second decade, but it seems reasonable to suppose that a high proportion of those born with both Chiron and Neptune in Pisces will develop these skills and view them as natural talents. Both Chiron and Neptune have been shown to be in prominent positions in the astrological charts of those working in the healing professions. Education systems that create avenues for children to express such talents may be much in demand.

Although there is evidence of the emergence of a new world order in 2012, it would be quite wrong to infer that the difficulties apparent in 2009 will be totally resolved by 2012. This year, however, should see a final winding down of the aggression of the previous years. Solar activity is likely to be increasing by this time too, bringing with it a growing need to accentuate the positive. The solar eclipses of 2012 are curious. There are two as opposed to the four of the previous year. The first, in the first degree of Gemini, accentuates the dawn of an information age quite unlike that which opened the millennium. The second, in November, may usher in new business practices. This wave of business change is unlikely to be completed until late 2014 but should prove pivotal. The older generation at this time could find the period confusing and, from their perspective, quite impractical. Yet there is evidence to suggest the emergence of new ways of doing business that focus more on the needs of all, and which seek to redress the acute imbalances between rich and poor states as defined at the beginning of the millennium. This suggests that the years 2013 to 2018 will be both poignant and market-changing.

2013–2018

The social, political and economic landscapes after 2013 promise to be very different from those of the early years of this new millennium. Certainly, the sun will still rise as it has always done and the shape of human beings will not have changed. But priorities will have changed – dramatically. Where nationality once held sway, a move towards humanism will gather pace. Increasingly, the effect that decisions taken in one part of the globe have on another will demand high levels of social accountability. Politicians should find this period challenging. In the short term, power vacuums could emerge. A Union of States of America might even devolve, leaving, for a short time, just one or two states holding the title of 'Super-power'. The five years from 2013 should be regarded as a time of transition following a period of great drama.

The end of the first decade of the millennium offers a platform for change. Global warfare is a distinct possibility, yet this is not the only possible outcome. The collapse of credit would have similarly devastating consequences – particularly in countries that have built up significant levels of debt. What takes place during 2010 will affect us all. It will surely take time for each and every one of us to absorb the enormity of events, and the years to 2013 could leave many people in a state of shock, so that the real transition into new modes of being might not begin until early that year.

Aside from the awesome planetary configuration of the period, Jupiter crosses backwards and forwards over the Aries point during 2010. This is highly unusual and has certainly not occurred in the last few centuries. The Aries point is defined as that place in the sky where the Sun makes its crossing from South to North latitude. The event takes place around 20–21 March each year. People all over the world are aware of the change in season around this time. The various orbits of the planets mean that they can align with this point at *any* date in the year. When the planet involved is relatively slow moving, taking perhaps more than a few days to make the crossing, the human race acquires a new way of looking at the world. While Jupiter has for long been the planet associated with wisdom, wisdom is not the same as common sense. There is no 'common denominator' at work. Wisdom is not necessarily democratic but demands an awareness of what is ethically and morally right. Religion plays a role here, so that it is entirely possible that the fracas of 2010 will involve hostilities between people of differing creeds. It is equally probable that the wisdom of an even higher authority will take a stronger grip in the hearts and minds of many people.

Significant change could come about through the dramatic change in attitude demanded as the cosmic storms of 2010 abate and new forces come into play. Growing awareness that we are all dependent on one another brings with it a change in commercial thinking. Jupiter's extended crossing

135

of the Aries point sows the seeds for the development of new ways of thinking. Commercial activity would be as affected as every other aspect of life. If Jupiter may be said to trigger intent, it takes the arrival of another planet on the scene to effect radical changes. That planet is often Uranus, whose moves from one sign to another so often coincide with progress via revolutionary change. In 2010, the orchestration of the cycles of the planets is awesome. Uranus moves across the Aries point more or less with Jupiter, although it is a further year before it gains authority in that sign. Change could, indeed, be fast and furious.

Anchoring these changes promises to be a saturnine task. It is likely to take until 5 October 2012 for new trading arrangements to be agreed. From this date, commercial arrangements between nations could follow a pattern very different from those of earlier years. It is true that a common feature of the end of wars is a determination to ensure that such events do not recur. The roots of global conflict in 2010 will no doubt be as complex as those of any war. I have described these as 'Water Wars' but they could just as easily be about oil, or the gap between rich and poor nations. What seems certain is that the conclusion of hostilities will embrace the need for reformation in social, economic and political authority. The initial stages of these transitions are likely to involve quick enthusiasms, which are eventually displaced by monumental shifts in attitudes, behaviour and authority.

From the economic perspective this is likely to be a short-term return to what were long considered to be traditional values. Hard currency – quite literally the use of precious metals and gems – will gain popularity. The fact that gold prices look set to soar throughout 2012 and 2013 certainly underlines a return to ownership of tangible commodities rather than the more nebulous values of equities and bonds. Far more revolutionary, however, will be the wiping out of large-scale debt. Unthinkable as this may be for many, it is likely to be the preferred solution for those, born in the mid-1960s, who by this time will be in positions of authority. This group of individuals will have no compunction about effecting change that is incomprehensible to others. It is even possible that this is one of the very reasons for their presence on the planet. It is, perhaps, only those born under that special alignment of Uranus and Pluto in Virgo who have the necessary imagination, determination, logic and intellect to effect change of the required magnitude. The extraordinary conjunction under which they were born will have moved through its quarter phase. They will have acquired maturity and experience and should have the confidence and stature to take their place as leaders.

Experienced investors born under other configurations may conclude that any speculation should remain at a cautious level. Those who have studied economic history should have no difficulty in identifying the widening financial fault-lines that open up in 2012. The solar eclipses of 2013, lying across the Taurus–Scorpio axis, mark times of re-evaluation and a return to basic values. Many people, aggrieved by the treatment meted out to them through banks and government pension agencies in the previous five years, may have resorted to hoarding, and storing 'cash under the mattress'. Others may have transferred their wealth to precious metals and jewels. Recalling that Venus will have made her second transit across the face of the Sun in 2012, it is probable that there will have been an increase in the value of these goods, with both emeralds and gold leading the way. Indeed, the value of these may have grown sharply throughout 2011 and 2012, but the rise is likely to be halted by the Taurus solar eclipse of 10 May 2013.

The idea that people might choose to 'go it alone' rather than entrust their cash to banks or building societies is underscored by the fact that, between 5 October 2012 and 23 December 2014, Saturn, from the geocentric perspective, passes through Scorpio. This transit is usually experienced negatively by the banking sector. During those periods when Venus joins Saturn in this sign, the expected fall in the value of these shares may be exaggerated. The two pronounced periods would be 26 November to 16 December 2012, and 11 September to 7 October 2013. Not every bank-stock would drop in value of course. Those stocks considered to be 'top of the range' and backed by full and professional support services could improve their standing, even if their share values do not rise until Saturn has moved perhaps as much as a sixth of the way around the zodiac. Once again, those banks which are not linked to national institutions could find that they make significant gains. Investors, then, should not balk from these stocks, but rather should be particularly selective in their choices.

A special planetary anniversary occurs around this time. The great Wall Street Crash took place during the last few weeks of October of 1929. From mid June 2012 until March 2013, Uranus will once more be passing over the degree of the zodiac it held then. This return of the planet to its position in 1929 might not pass unnoticed given that several of the slow-moving planets will also be making contact with the important degrees active in 1929. If trading reaction to these degrees occurs on the same level as it did all those years ago, this particular period could prove exceedingly difficult.

A reduction in the number of hostile take-overs is probable in 2012 and

137

2013. Indeed, it may be that even the concept of take-overs becomes frowned upon. Increased encouragement and support for those trying to achieve market standing is more likely, with small and medium-sized retail businesses enjoying periods of cautious optimism. After long periods of both shortage and trading difficulty these businesses look poised to advance. Whilst it may not be until 2014 that significant profits are made once more, those firms able to join the marketplace in 2012 should find faith in their products confirmed by demand. Those who back these enterprises could realise benefits relatively quickly.

Neither Mercury nor Venus is ever far from the Sun. The former can never be more than approximately 28 degrees from it, whilst the latter is never more than 78 degrees from our central star (viewed geocentrically). If the position of the Moon is added to our view of the solar system, there is a high probability, during any year, that clusters of planets will occur within the space of just 20 degrees of the zodiac. Emphasis on a particular area goes some way towards explaining a concentration of energy. This is hugely important in the marketplace. The dominance of particular industry sectors over a period of months is fairly normal. It is rare to have long periods when there is no such concentration of energy. Yet these conditions will exist from late in 2014 until 2019. Such a lack of emphasis suggests that no one sector will be at an advantage throughout these years. Indeed, it may be that all sectors will make strides.

In general terms, a period of appreciation of craftsmanship is suggested between 2013 and 2018. This could prove a time of renaissance, with increased attention given to the role of the artisan. Colours, sounds and scents come into their own during this time too, and firms able to provide quality items under any or all of these guises should be considered for investment. As these years might cover a period of maximum sunspot activity, high levels of creativity are to be expected.

If planet cycles continue to act as they have done in the past, then 2014 will be a year of intense difficulty for the US administration. A collapse in government is probable. This might in part be due to the need to raise taxes to cover costs incurred during the 'Water Wars' period. If the Union of States were to collapse, this would, of course, have an impact on trade across the world and be a contributory factor in falls in the American trade indices of the latter half of 2014. Under such conditions, recovery world-wide could take some considerable time. There are many indications to suggest that 2015 will be a period of unease – at least from the economic perspective.

Further advances in both science and technology are indicated in the first weeks of the year and the positive vibrations these bring may encourage an upward move within some sectors. Even so, Uranus and Pluto will still be at right-angles to one another. Those who respond to this influence will be in a more negative frame of mind.

The exact angle (geocentric) takes place on 17 March 2015, and within days there is an important solar eclipse (20 March), within a few hours of the Sun reaching the Aries, or 'human race', point. This eclipse is total but will only be visible across the Arctic. Even so, it could have a very real effect on human behaviour. It takes place on a Friday and at a time when all the European markets will be open for trade. It also lies on the midpoint between Mercury and Mars. During the times in each trading day when these two planets take up a prominent position over the stock exchanges of the world, activity (volume of trade) tends to increase. The relationship between these two planets, the eclipse and the Aries point, suggests something of a market storm. It is, of course, possible that a natural calamity could occur and that this will trigger exaggerated reaction. The trading week of 16–20 March should be treated with some caution.

Nor should it be assumed that once this week is over economic storms will abate. With several planets moving into square formation in the succeeding months, 2015 could prove volatile and exhausting for traders trying to gauge each wave of activity. In May particularly, a depression could hit various indices. It may be September before calmer conditions are experienced. From then on, and for some months into 2016, there should be improvement.

Difficulties may await, however. It would be as well to monitor the last few days of June carefully. Jupiter and Pluto will be working towards holding a pattern where they are just a third of a cycle apart. This is often seen as a positive signal. However, on 28 June 2016, a curious pattern forms that may signal serious negative pressure. It could be the first week of July before recovery begins. By this time, Mars will be appearing to move forward after some weeks of apparent retrograde motion, and Mercury's relationship with the two larger planets becomes more prominent. These factors suggest a bounce after a fall.

Saturn will have made its Sagittarius ingress during 2015 and pressure will no doubt have fallen once more on the travel industry, though this cannot really be compared to the difficulties this industry experienced in the wake of 11 September 2001. Improved journey times, as a result of advances in both design and available fuels, coupled with stringent security arrangements, should have curtailed earlier difficulties. Even so, many companies working in this sector could face tough times. Perhaps because there will be a more robust international community setting standards, some planes may be grounded. Awareness of the pollution caused by their fuel systems, and suggestions that some of the machines are now too dangerous to fly, could easily result in certain businesses being permanently grounded. Investors will need to take great care that the companies that seem to offer exciting growth are not, in fact, affected by losses incurred in previous years which make for uncomfortable reading on the relevant balance sheets.

Saturn is due to pass over the Galactic Centre point in May 2017. Such a transit has, in the past, been consistent with spectacular market falls, and investors will wish to keep a wary weather eye on events leading into this month. It so happens that this event takes place close to several stock-market 'birthdays' – dates when, consciously or unconsciously, markets want to rise. The Tokyo, Wall Street and Johannesburg markets fit into this group. This Galactic Centre crossing is markedly different from those of earlier times, however. During this period Saturn and Uranus will have travelled a third of a cycle from one another. This has proved to be a constructive angle with regard to economic activity. When the two planets formed this alignment in 1913, 1926 and 1956, there were sustained periods of prosperity. There is room then for cautious optimism.

Indeed, it is quite possible that the real force of changes in attitude that develop after 2011 will be obvious in May 2017, so it is possible that the world will escape a repeat of the traumas that usually occur when Saturn crosses the Galactic Centre.

2018–2020

The end of the period under review promises to be no less exciting and challenging than the start. In a very real sense 2020 promises to be the dawn of a new age. This may in no small part be due to the influence of a superior cycle chronicled from ancient times. Jupiter and Saturn form a conjunction every twenty years; over a period of approximately 180 years, successive conjunctions occur in a particular 'type' of sign, be it Fire, Earth, Air or Water. This extended cycle broadly coincides with social changes that are mirrored by variations in approach to financial management. An 'Earth' period matches a time when people save before spending; an 'Air' period promises a rather different attitude – one that puts spending first.

The conjunction forming in 2020 will be the first of an 'Air' series that continues until the year 2159. This 'first-in-the-series conjunction' marks a 'seed' moment – a moment when new ideas emerge. It is a time for fresh beginnings. Any 'Air' series focuses on ideas, taking priority over the more practical approach. Notwithstanding the trials of the previous two decades, individuals coming of age in 2020 may be all too eager to embark on adventures that eventually see an escalation in the use of complex financial instruments not dissimilar to the rise of derivative trading in the 1980s. The opportunities for this group to explore new areas of financial management may be plentiful. Although, by 2020, the number of currencies is likely to have reduced substantially, and further technological advancements will have rendered certain transactions obsolete, the ethereal nature of trades not based on tangible currency, but rather on ideas, will give rise to variations on derivative trading in keeping with the age. The year 2020 is likely to be the true dawn of smart card financial management even if history shows the first recorded use of these implements to have occurred some forty years earlier.

From 1802 to 2000, with the exception of just one conjunction, the alignments of Jupiter and Saturn took place in Earth signs. The odd-one-out of the cycle occurred in 1981 in the Air sign of Libra. The financial attitudes and behaviour of traders of that period afforded a glimpse of the future and the attitudes that would hold sway in 2020. Around 1981, the word 'yuppie' was introduced into our vocabulary; this too was the period when derivatives – the extraordinary financial tools of economic whizz-kids – gained momentum. Long before the emergence of the 'dot-com' era, there was a surge in the number of credit transactions. The sheer number of young people owning credit cards, through which they could incur large-scale debt, astounded those of earlier generations whose financial management was based on saving before spending and whose sole debt tended to take the form of a mortgage.

In the closing stages of the 1981 cycle, and with the Earth conjunction of 2000 looming on the horizon, words such as 'prudence' and 'savings' were uttered loudly by politicians and bankers as it became clear that debts threatened to become unmanageable. Older values were recalled, though many financial advisors felt these warnings to be 'too little, too late'. The year 2000 marked the end of a longer cycle, the closing phases of which were to prove painful for some who had extended themselves. The meeting of Jupiter and Saturn in May 2000 resulted in a rare and fascinating planet formation that included both Uranus and Neptune. Volatility in the marketplace was evident. Financial alarm bells were sounded loud and clear though not, it seems, heeded by everyone. Many investors fell at the May 2000 hurdle. Others toppled a little later.

Further casualties may be expected – particularly when the two planets oppose one another at the end of the first decade of the 21st century. Between 2010 and 2011, those who were deaf to early warnings will be served a short, sharp reminder of the price to be paid for excessive risk-taking. Whilst a 1930s-type depression could yet be avoided, there is much to suggest that, at the very least, the early 2010s will require that individuals practise prudent financial management. Credit is unlikely to be widely available again until 2018. That said, the concerted efforts made by a number of confident individuals prepared to 'do business differently' may be successful, so that by the end of 2017, cautious optimism should be apparent in many quarters. Equities could be moving forwards slowly but steadily, and once again there may be talk of gains through investment. Even some of those who suffered at the end of the first decade may decide that there is more to be gained through equity investment than by saving at the local bank.

This period will also find those born in the 1990s ready to take their first steps as investors. Despite the fact that their childhoods may have been marred by hostility between nations and the collapse of the credit bubble, many of these young individuals could be tempted into investing anew. They will bring with them great enthusiasm and a willingness to invest in areas far away from their native locale. The sums most have at their disposal may be small, but their ability to home in on activities that bring swift reward could be fascinating. The commercial instincts of this group may be a factor in the move towards global trading that is very different from that of twenty years earlier.

By 2019, the political spectrum could be radically different from that of the early years of the 21st century. A shift in power and authority is probable. Even the most cursory look at planetary trends affecting the USA suggests that the American nation will no longer exist in its present form. The recognised shift from West to East, as determined by successive Neptune–Pluto conjunctions, will probably be blatantly apparent. So too may be the emergence of a new trading bloc of states in the African continent. Certainly the solar eclipse scheduled for 21 June 2020 – a solstice – places Uranus proud in the sky over central Africa and would appear to mark surging levels of commercial activity in this region. Indeed, there is little reason to suppose that the 'dark continent' will *not* enjoy a central role on the world stage after 2020.

The meeting of Jupiter and Saturn in 2020 would have been termed a 'Grand Mutation' by the ancients. This term describes a shift by these two planets from one series to another. This Grand Mutation is special in another sense, however. The meeting of the two planets is scheduled for 21 December and takes place within hours of the solstice – one of the four most important points of the natural year. The implications of this coincidence suggest that the weeks either side of this occurrence will be eventful – even dramatic. The stage may be set not just by the solar eclipse of the earlier solstice, but by two other cycles that come to their 'start' points earlier in the year.

Both Jupiter and Saturn form conjunctions with Pluto in January 2020. Their scheduled appointments take place in the 'business' or corporate sign of Capricorn. The correlation between this cycle and outbreaks of violence between ancient peoples has already been noted. It is, indeed, possible that hostilities may once again break out between Arab and Israeli, Hindu and Moslem, etc. However, given all that will have occurred in the previous years, it is just as possible that some, or perhaps all, will be restrained from such action by a global authority. It is interesting that Jupiter makes its conjunction with Pluto just weeks after Saturn's meeting with the latter planet. Could it be that arbitration and conciliation will be the order of the day? Wisdom could yet triumph over precedent. Certainly, the latter combination of planets indicates growth and the desire to move forward.

This attitude could prevail in commercial activities also. Saturn's alignment with Pluto at the start of the year implies a hard attitude to business affairs. Under this planet formation, every effort is made to pare costs, to minimise the need for credit, and to husband resources. Saturn will be travelling through its 'own' sign: this time accenting family businesses. It will be interesting to note how many such ventures are launched during this period. This looks to be the age of the true entrepreneur whose foray into trading is driven by the need to protect and secure both immediate and extended family. The necessary capital for these ventures may be found through those same groups whose desire is to support and nurture the creativity within. This suggests a return to Confucian principles. Indeed, we might expect the wisdom of such masters to dominate many newspaper articles as the Chinese New Year approaches in February 2020. Conservative attitudes are likely to prevail with few wishing to indulge in business plans that imply rapid growth. This, though, could prove to be an error of judgment.

The Saturn brakes are released within weeks, as Jupiter moves to make its conjunction with Pluto. Jupiter's pressure on the commercial accelerator should see a rapid expansion. Within just a short time the goods and services launched at the start of the year gather momentum. An upsurge in trading suggests a sharp rise both in volume and price in the equity markets. Many will feel they are on the crest of a new wave. Words of caution may be ringing in their ears, yet few will be able to deny the clear potential for growth. The fundamental balancing act between conserving resources and good husbandry on the one hand versus seizing the moment and capitalising on opportunities on the other, looks poised to challenge even the most experienced of Chief Executives. The second quarter of the year promises a steady but clear rise in global indices that continues until the solstice eclipse on 21 June. By the time the Sun reappears from behind the Moon that day, even those who feel they are experienced in the ways of the world could agree that a new world order is emerging.

The conflict between old ways of working and new ways of thinking should exercise the minds of many in 2020. Where the start of the year finds a yearning towards the politics and social structures of earlier times, its ending finds a leaning towards innovative systems. For much of the previous two hundred or more years, politicians and economists were encouraged to learn from earlier judgments. Resort to historical precedent is unlikely to work as 2020 draws to a close. The imperative, then, is to ride on the crest of a new wave bringing with it a new approach to politics and finance. The perfect stage for this lies in an international institution that, even in 2020, will still be in its infancy.

Elsewhere it has been indicated that the United Nations would probably give way to a global forum launched not too long after Pluto crosses the Galactic Centre point (2007). The first few years of this new organisation are likely to be very tense. As with its predecessors, the League of Nations and United Nations, it may seem inadequate or badly formed. Its constitution may be felt by some to be too idealistic. Yet we will be moving into a new age. Taken in isolation, the Grand Mutation suggests the beginning of a new phase where military conflict is replaced by wars of words and high-level debate.

This factor cannot be considered alone. By 2020, Pluto will have journeyed through much of the sign of Capricorn. Pluto challenges us to let go of out-worn ideals. Exhausting and challenging as this can be, it is also an essential part of the process that permits new ideas to surface. For at least the last few thousand years, 'nationality' has been an acceptable concept. Many people feel a particular affinity with a special area of the world and truly value this connection. This has been both a blessing and a curse. Often, the protection of national boundaries has been claimed as a justification for war. Over the next two decades a shift towards accepting that there will have to be jurisdiction within trading zones could lead to a reduction in the number of national boundaries. Trading zones may have to take priority over these smaller geographic areas as the global village becomes a reality for all.

In the opening chapter we considered our relationship to the cosmos, and the legacy of ancients who recognised a link between the stars and specific locations. Across the globe there are numerous man-made and natural features that synchronise with specific star placements. The links are astonishing. One of the best examples is the link between the three stars Mintaka, Alnilam and Alnitak (forming Orion's Belt) and the pyramids of ancient Egypt. Even the internal shafts of these pyramids may be shown to point to star constellations. The ancients found meaning in this relationship. It is entirely possible that in the space of the next twenty years, as man's interest in the heavens grows, inspired by the work achieved by astrophysicists, there will be a concerted effort to step up the quest to decode this language.

The stars rotate around a central pole. Around 2080, they will return to positions held approximately 26,000 years ago. As with the seconds on a clock, time is ticking by. We are now within 'minutes' of this return. When it happens, the alignment of sacred sites and stars will be spectacular. We cannot know if some higher authority will see this as a moment to return to Earth. What we can know is that there is little time left for us to learn this ancient language. If this timing has been put in place by some higher intelligence then decoding any message left for us would surely serve us well. An early step along the way would be for us to understand the language of the cycles of the planets, the rhythms of the Sun, and the relevance of our special place in the universe.

Notes

chapter 1   The Changing Sky

1   Earth speed:
    http://whatis.techtarget.com/definition/0,,sid9_gci849653,00.html.
2   Lt Cmdr David Williams, *Financial Astrology* (American Federation of Astrologers, 1982), p. 98.
3   Bayeux Tapestry: www.bayeuxtapestry.org.uk.
4   Dambuster Raid: www.dambusters.org.uk/damsops.htm.
5   Solar information from:
    www.museum.vic.gov.au/planetarium/solarsystem/sun.html.
6   Earth Distance Travelled:
    http://spacelink.nasa.gov/Instructional.Materials/Curriculum.Support/
    Space.Science/Our.Solar.System/.
7   Solar Flares: http://hesperia.gsfc.nasa.gov/sftheory/flare.htm.
8   Williams, *Financial Astrology*, p. 39.
9   William Houston, *Through The Whirlwind* (Little, Brown and Company, 1997), p. 11.
10 William Houston, *Riding the Business Cycle* (Little, Brown and Company, 1995), p. 17.
11 Ibid., p. 18.
12 Sun Spot Activity: Neil F. Michelsen, *Tables of Planetary Phenomena* (ACS Publications Inc., 1990), p. 206.
13 Solar Storm:
    http://www.space.com/scienceastronomy/solar_flare_031028.html.
14 RWC Belgium World Data Centre for the Sunspot Index:
    http://sidc.oma.be/index.php3.
15 Sunspot Information: www.spaceweather.com/java/sunspot.html.
16 Sunspots: http://science.nasa.gov/ssl/pad/solar/sunspots.htm.
17 Maunder Minimum:
    http://www.eso.org/gen-fac/libraries/lisa3/beckmanj.html.
18 Number of Sunspots: www.colorado-research.com
19 William Houston, *Riding the Business Cycle*, p. 10.
20 Michelsen, *Tables of Planetary Phenomena*, p. 198.
21 Ibid., p. 14.
22 Michelsen, *Tables of Planetary Phenomena*, p. 14.

23   Daily Sunspot Information: www.spaceweather.com/java/sunspot.html.

chapter 2   Stars and Sacred Places

1   Mark Vidler, *The Star Mirror* (Thorsons, 1999), p. 66.
2   Patrick Moore, *Philip's Guide to Stars and Planets* (Chancellor Press, 2002), p. 178.
3   Bernadette Brady, *Brady's Book of Fixed Stars* (Weiser, 1998), p. 206.
4   Arthur P. Norton, *NORTON'S STAR ATLAS and Reference Handbook* (Gall & Inglis Ltd.; John Wiley & Sons, New York, 1986).
5   Brady, *Brady's Book of Fixed Stars*, p. 207.
6   B. A. Phythian and L. C. Pascoe, *Encyclopaedia of Dates and Events* (Hodder & Stoughton, 1991), p. 413.
7   Mark Vidler, *The Star Mirror* (Thorsons, 1999), p. 74.
8   Thomas G. Shanks, *The International Atlas Second Edition* (ACS Publications Ltd, 1988), p. 135.
9   Positions calculated using Starlight Software (Zyntara Publications, 2003).
10 Brady, *Brady's Book of Fixed Stars*, p. 195.
11 Positions calculated using Starlight Software.
12 Brady, *Brady's Book of Fixed Stars*, p. 81.
13 Dr Marc Edmund Jones, *Sabian Symbols* (Aurora Press, 1993).

chapter 3   World Trade and Planet Cycles

1   The Smithsonian National Air and Space Museum: www.nasm.sc.edu.
2   Michael Baigent, Nicholas Campion and Charles Harvey, *Mundane Astrology* (The Aquarian Press, 1984), p. 177.
3   Neil F. Michelsen, *Tables of Planetary Phemonena* (ACS Publications Inc., 1990), p. 90.
4   Ibid.
5   Ibid.
6   Calculated using software by Herschel (Cambridge, 1998).
7   *Tables of Planetary Phemonena*, p. 90.
8   Ibid.
9   Ibid.
10 Solar Fire software, Esoteric Technologies Pty Ltd 1994–2001, version 5.0.24.
11 Ibid.
12 James Trager,*The People's Chronology* (Aurum Press Ltd, 1992), p. 196.
13 Ibid.
14 Ibid., p. 197.
15 Ibid., p. 198.
16 Calculated using software by Herschel.
17 James Trager, *The People's Chronology* (Aurum Press Ltd, 1992), p. 240.
18 Ibid., p. 241.
19 Calculated using software by Herschel.

20 James Trager, *The People's Chronology* (Aurum Press Ltd, 1992), p. 382.
21 Ibid., p. 388.
22 Ibid.
23 Calculated using software by Herschel.
24 James Trager, *The People's Chronology*, p. 207.
25 Ibid.
26 Calculated using software by Herschel.
27 Ibid.
28 Gapper and Denton, *All That Glitters* (Penguin, 1996), p. 29.
29 Christeen Skinner Data Collection.
30 Solar Fire software, Esoteric Technologies Pty Ltd 1994–2001, version 5.0.24.
31 Ibid.

chapter 4 Forecasting

1 *The Sunday Times*, 2 April 2000.
2 Neil F. Michelsen, *Tables of Planetary Phenomena* (ACS Publications Inc., 1990), p. 90.
3 Ibid., p. 90.
4 W. D. Gann, *45 Years in Wall St.* (Lambert Gann, 1949), p. 60.
5 John Steele Gordon, *The Great Game* (Orion Business Books, 1999), p. 160.
6 William Houston, *Through The Whirlwind* (Little, Brown and Co., 1997), p. 13.
7 Michelson, *Tables of Planetary Phenomena*, p. 91 .
8 The Love Bug: http://news.bbc.co.uk/1/hi/uk/736080.stm.
9 Michael Baigent, Nicholas Campion and Charles Harvey, *Mundane Astrology* (The Aquarian Press, 1984), p. 336.
10 Ibid.
11 Redundancies: http://news.bbc.co.uk/1/hi/business/1286932.stm.
12 Calculated using software by Herschel (Cambridge, 1998).
13 Baigent, Campion and Harvey, *Mundane Astrology*, p. 183.
14 Calculated using software by Herschel.
15 Transit of Venus: http://www.vt-2004.org/.
16 Michelson, *Tables of Planetary Phenomena*, p. 91.
17 Ibid.

chapter 5 Transformation

1 B. A. Phythian and L. C. Pascoe, *Encyclopaedia of Dates and Events* (Hodder & Stoughton, 1968), p. 587.

chapter 6 Collapse of the USA

1 Nicholas Campion, *The Book of World Horoscopes* (Cinnabar Books, 1995), p. 405.
2 Ibid., p. 110.

3   Patrick Moore, *Philip's Guide to Stars and Planets* (Chancellor Press, 2002), p. 64.
4   Neil F. Michelsen, *Tables of Planetary Phenomena* (ACS Publications Inc., 1990), p. 64.
5   James Trager, *The People's Chronology* (Aurum, 1992), p. 791.
6   Yamomoto Quote: http://www.worldhistory.com/wiki/I/Isoroku-Yamamoto's-sleeping-giant-quote.htm.
7   USA President Inauguration Date:
    http://www.annieshomepage.com/inauguration.html.
8   President Ford Inauguration:
    http://www.galleryofhistory.com/archive/12_2003/presidents.
9   Ibid.
10 George W. Bush Birth data: http://www.astrodatabank.com.
11 President George W. Bush Inugauration:
    http://www.yale.edu/lawweb/avalon/presiden/inaug/gbush1.htm.
12 Neil Michelsen, *Tables of Planetary Phenomena*, p. 66.
13 Jim Lewis and Ariel Guttman, *The Astro*Carto*Graphy Book of Maps* (Llewellyn Publications, 1989), p. 179.
14 Ibid., p. 175.
15 President Wilson Anti-Trust Legislation:
    http://www.u-s-history.com/pages/h1056.html.
16 President Wilson Laws:
    http://www.whitehouse.gov/history/presidents/ww28.html.
17 Ibid.
18 President Truman quote to reporters:
    http://www.multied.com/Bio/presidents/truman.html.
19 Ibid.
20 President Wilson Acts:
    http://www.americaslibrary.gov/cgi-bin/page.cgi/jb/modern/fairdeal.
21 President Ford Inauguration:
    http://www.ford.utexas.edu/library/speeches/740001.htm.
22 Trager, *The People's Chronology*, p. 380.
23 John Steele Gordon, *The Great Game* (Orion Business Books, 1999), p. 66.
24 Ibid., p. 64.
25 Ibid., p. 66.
26 Ibid., p. 194.

chapter 7   The World Bank

1   James Trager, *The People's Chronology* (Aurum, 1992), p. 889.
2   Catherine Caulfield, *Masters of Illusion* (Pan, 1996), p. 45.
3   Ibid.
4   Neil F. Michelsen, *Tables of Planetary Phenomena* (ACS Publications Inc., 1990), p. 204.
5   Ibid.

6   David Ovason, *The Book of the Eclipse* (Arrow, 1999).
7   Joan McEvers, *Spiritual, Metaphysical & New Trends in Modern Astrology* (Llewellyn, 1988), p. 181.
8   Ibid., p. 164.
9   Catherine Caulfield, *Masters of Illusion* (Pan, 1996), p. 42.
10 Ibid., p. 170.
11 Ibid., p. 70.
12 Ibid., p. 73.
13 Ibid., p. 10.
14 Ibid., p. 10.
15 Ibid., p. 11.

chapter 8   The Credit Bubble and Currency Crisis

1   Neil F. Michelsen, *Tables of Planetary Phenomena* (ACS Publications Inc., 1990), p. 14.
2   Patrick Moore, *Philip's Guide to Stars and Planets* (Chancellor Press, 2002), p. 63.
3   Ibid., p. 53.
4   Ibid., p. 56.
5   http://news.bbc.co.uk/1/hi/business/the_economy/159082.stm.
6   John Steele Gordon, *The Great Game* (Orion Business Books, 1999), p. 194.
7   Alan Greenspan birth data:
    http://abcnews.go.com/reference/bios/greenspan.html.
8   Gold price data: http://www.globalfindata.com.
9   Ibid.

chapter 9   Water Wars, 2010

1   Nicholas Campion, *The Book of World Horoscopes* (Cinnabar Books, 1995), p. 208.
2   *Chronicle of the 20th Century* (Longman, 1998).
3   Ibid., p. 1208.
4   Ibid.
5   Ibid., p. 1068.
6   Ibid., p. 1069.
7   Ibid., p. 1078.
8   Ibid., p. 528.
9   Michael Baigent, Nicholas Campion and Charles Harvey, *Mundane Astrology* (The Aquarian Press, 1984), p. 388.
10 Ibid., p. 277.
11 Ibid.
12 Baigent, Campion and Harvey, *Mundane Astrology*, p. 177.
13 B. A. Phythian and L. C. Pascoe, *Encyclopaedia of Dates and Events* (Hodder & Stoughton, 1968), p. 413.
14 Baigent, Campion and Harvey, *Mundane Astrology*, p. 192.
15 Clifford Data Collection via Solar Fire Technologies.
16 *Chronicle of the 20th Century*, p. 951.

17   Ibid., pp. 929 and p. 930.
18   Ibid., p. 929.
19   Ibid., p. 935.
20   Ibid., p. 935.
21   Ibid., p. 939.
22   Ibid., p. 943.
23   Ibid., p. 947.
24   Ibid., p. 957.
25   Michael Munkasey, *Midpoints* (ACS Publications, 1991), p. 398.
26   Ibid.
27   James Trager, *The People's Chronology* (Aurum, 1992), p. 1102.
28   *Chronicle of the 20th Century*, p. 1276.
29   Ibid., p. 1096.
30   Ibid., p. 1096.
31   Phythian and Pascoe, *Encyclopaedia of Dates and Events*, p. 397.
32   Ibid., p. 396.
33   Ibid.
34   James Trager, *The People's Chronology*, p. 538.
35   Campion, *The Book of World Horoscopes*.
36   Ibid., p. 199.

chapter 10   Illusions and Imagination

1   B. A. Phythian and L. C. Pascoe, *Encyclopaedia of Dates and Events* (Hodder & Stoughton, 1968), p. 477.
2   *The New Harvard Dictionary of Music* (Belknap Harvard, 1986), p. 84.
3   Phythian and Pascoe, *Encyclopaedia of Dates and Events*ton, 1968), p. 469.
4   Ibid., p. 471.
5   Ibid., p. 470.
6   James Trager, *The People's Chronology* (Aurum, 1992), p. 421.
7   Phythian and Pascoe, *Encyclopaedia of Dates and Events*, p. 471.
8   Ibid., p. 475.
9   James Trager, *The People's Chronology*, p. 437.
10   Phythian and Pascoe, *Encyclopaedia of Dates and Events*, p. 479.
11   Trager, *The People's Chronology*, p. 447.
12   Phythian and Pascoe, *Encyclopaedia of Dates and Events*, p. 483.
13   Trager, *The People's Chronology*, p. 447.
14   Ibid., p. 464.
15   Ibid., p. 486.

chapter 12   Wall Street and London Markets, 2004–2020

1   Transit of Venus: www.venus-transit.de.
2   Sousa: http://www.sunearth.gsfc.nasa.gov.

3   James Trager, *The People's Chronology* (Aurum, 1992), pp. 239.

4   Ibid., pp. 307–14.

5   Ibid., pp. 530–64.

6   Gold price data: www.globalfindata.com.

7   John Steele Gordon, *The Great Game* (Orion Business Books, 1999), p. 226.

8   Trager, *The People's Chronology*, p. 775.

9   Nicholas Campion, *Book of World Horoscopes* (Cinnabar Books, 1995), p. 393.

10   William Houston, *Riding the Business Cycle* (Little, Brown & Co, 1995), p. 111.

11   B. A. Phythian and L. C. Pascoe, *Encyclopaedia of Dates and Events* (Hodder & Stoughton, 1968), p. 399.

12   Ibid., p. 401.

13   Trager, *The People's Chronology*, p. 305.

14   Ibid., p. 1009.

15   Houston, *Riding the Business Cycle*, p. 162.

16   Trager, *The People's Chronology*, p. 1009.

17   Ibid.

18   Martin S. Fridson, *It Was a Very Good Year* (Wiley & Sons, 1998), p. 29.

19   John Steele Gordon, *The Great Game*, p. 203.

20   Theodor Landscheidt, *Sun*Earth*Man* (Urania Trust, 1989), p. 28.

21   Trager, *The People's Chronology*, p. 175.

22   Phythian and Pascoe, *Encyclopaedia of Dates and Events*, p. 649.

Throughout *The Financial Universe*, the position of the planets have been calculated using the software: Solar Fire, Esoteric Technologies Pty Technologies Pty Ltd 1994–2001, version 5.0.24; and Herschel software (Cambridge, 1998), c/o the author.

Bibliography

Facts and figures

The New Harvard Dictionary of Music (Belknap Harvard, 1986).

Chronicle of the 20th Century (Longman, 1988).

Michelson, Neil, *Tables of Planetary Phenomena* (ACS Publications, Inc. 1990)

Norton, Arthur P., *NORTON'S STAR ATLAS and Reference Handbook* (Gall & Inglis Ltd.; John Wiley & Sons, New York, 1986)

Phythian, B. A. and Pascoe, L. C., *Encyclopaedia of Dates and Events* (Hodder & Stoughton, 1991).

Shanks, Thomas G., *The International Atlas Second Edition* (ACS Publications Ltd, 1988).

Trager, James, *The People's Chronology* (Aurum Press Ltd, 1992).

Financial data and references

Caulfield, Catherine, *Masters of Illusion* (Pan, 1996).

Houston, William, *Through The Whirlwind* (Little, Brown and Company, 1997).

Houston, William *Riding the Business Cycle* (Little, Brown and Company, 1995).

Gapper, John and Denton, Nicholas, *All That Glitters* (Penguin, 1996) .

Gann, W. D., *45 Years in Wall St.* (Lambert Gann, 1949).

Gordon, John Steele, *The Great Game* (Orion Business Books, 1999).

Fridson, Martin S., *It Was a Very Good Year,* (Wiley & Sons, 1998).

Williams, David, *Financial Astrology* (American Federation of Astrologers, 1982)

Astronomic and astrological references

Baigent, Michael, Campion, Nicholas, and Harvey, Charles, *Mundane Astrology* (The Aquarian Press, 1984).

Brady, Bernadette, *Brady's Book of Fixed Stars* (Weiser, 1998).

Campion, Nicholas, *The Book of World Horoscopes* (Cinnabar Books, 1995).

Landscheidt, Theodor, *Sun – Earth – Man* (Urania Trust, 1989) .

Lewis and Guttman, *The Astro*Carto*Graphy Book of Map* (Llewellyn Publications, 1989).

Jones, Dr Marc Edmund, *Sabian Symbols* (Aurora Press, 1993).

McEvers, Joan *Spiritual, Metaphysical & New Trends in Modern Astrology* (Llewellyn, 1988).

Moore, Patrick, *Philip's Guide to Stars and Planets* (Chancellor Press, 2002).

Munkasey, Michael, *Midpoints* (ACS Publications Inc., 1991).

Bibliography

Ovason, David, *The Book of the Eclipse* (Arrow, 1999).
Vidler, Mark, *The Star Mirror* (Thorsons, 1999).

Website references

Astronomy resources

Earth speed : http://whatis.techtarget.com/definition/0,,sid9_gci849653,00.html

Solar information from various sites:

http://www.museum.vic.gov.au/planetarium/solarsystem/sun.html
http://spacelink.nasa.gov/Instructional.Materials/Curriculum.Support/Space.Science/
　　Our.Solar.System/
http://hesperia.gsfc.nasa.gov/sftheory/flare.htm
http://www.space.com/scienceastronomy/solar_flare_031028.html

Sunspot information from:

RWC Belgium World Data Centre for the Sunspot Index at
http://sidc.oma.be/index.php3
http://www.spaceweather.com/java/sunspot.html
http://science.nasa.gov/ssl/pad/solar/sunspots.htm
Maunder Minimum: http://www.eso.org/gen-fac/libraries/lisa3/beckmanj.html
The Smithsonian National Air and Space Museum: http://www.nasm.sc.edu
Transit of Venus: http://www.vt-2004.org/

Financial Resources

Gold price data: http://www.globalfindata.com

United States of America Presidents, Inaugural Speeches and Birth Data Resources

USA President Inauguration Date:
　　http://www.annieshomepage.com/inauguration.html

President Ford Inauguration:
　　http://www.galleryofhistory.com/archive/12_2003/presidents

President George W. Bush Inugauration: http://www.yale.edu/lawweb/avalon/pres-
iden/inaug/gbush1.htm

President Wilson Anti-Trust Legislation: http://www.u-s-
history.com/pages/h1056.html

President Wilson Laws: http://www.whitehouse.gov/history/presidents/ww28.html

President Truman quote to reporters:
　　http://www.multied.com/Bio/presidents/truman.html

President Wilson Acts: http://www.americaslibrary.gov/cgi-
bin/page.cgi/jb/modern/fairdeal

Bibliography

President Ford Inauguration:
  http://www.ford.utexas.edu/library/speeches/740001.htm
  http://news.bbc.co.uk/1/hi/business/the_economy/159082.stm
Alan Greenspan Birth Data: http://abcnews.go.com/reference/bios/greenspan.html
George W. Bush Birth Data: http://www.astrodatabank.com

Miscellaneous

Bayeux Tapestry: http://www.bayeuxtapestry.org.uk
Dambuster Raid: http://www.dambusters.org.uk/damsops.htm
Yamomoto Quote: http://www.worldhistory.com/wiki/I/Isoroku-Yamamoto's-sleeping-giant-quote.htm

Software

Throughout *The Financial Universe* the position of the planets were calculated using the software:
Solar Fire, Esoteric Technologies Pty Technologies Pty Ltd 1994–2001, version 5.0.24; and Herschel software (Cambridge, 1998), c/o the author.

Index

9/11 terrorist attack, 31, 50

advertising, 97, 98, 99, 113–14, 118
Afghanistan, 48, 51, 82, 92
ageing process, 99
airline industry, 31, 38, 114, 140
Alnilam, 145
Alnitak, 145
alternative medical practices, 129
anaesthesia, 100, 101, 102, 133
angina pectoris, 101
Angola, 87
anti-terrorist devices, 38–9
apartheid, 90
Apple, 27
Aquarius
    associations, 99
    passage of Neptune, 74, 95–6, 98–9,
      100–1
    passage of Pluto, 36
    passage of Sun, 49
    passage of Uranus, 94, 105
    traits of those born under, 98
Argentina, 82, 84
Aries, 79, 80, 89
    associations, 108
    passage of Neptune, 96
    passage of Uranus, 104, 106, 107–10
Aries point, 135–6, 139
art, 98–9, 111–12, 120
Ascella, 16
asteroids, 4, 5
atomic particles, 109–10
Australia, housing market, 41

Baigent, Michael, 33
Balkans, 9, 88
Bangladesh, 92

banking industry, 39–40
    computer virus, 29
    stock market activity, 114–15, 117, 121,
      123, 129, 130–1, 132, 137
    see also World Bank
Barycentre, 9
bassoon, 99
Bayeaux Tapestry, 3
BBC, 109
Beirut, 82, 87
Berlin Wall, fall of, 9, 90
Bernadette of Lourdes, 103
Bhutan, 92
Big Bang, 72
biochemistry, 102–3, 105
biotechnology industries, 107, 113, 114, 119
birth moment, 1–2
Bizet, Georges, 112
Black Hole M-82, 62
Blair, Tony, 7
blue-chip industries, 42, 117, 119, 132
Bolivia, 84
boom and bust rhythms, 23, 28, 35, 56–7
Borodin, Alexander, 112
Brahms, Johannes, 112
brain
    drugs development, 99
    knowledge, 101
    protection of, 100–1
brainwave companies, 101
Brazil, slavery, 21
Brenner, Sydney, 133
Bretton Woods conference, 61–5, 66
broadcasting, 109
building societies, 39, 117, 137
Burma, 92
Bush, George W., 7, 49–51, 53–4
Calcutta, 88

Index

Campion, Nicholas, 33
Canada
    birth-date, 45
    housing market, 41
Cancer, 80
    associations, 114, 116, 117
    Neptune–Pluto cycle, 18
    passage of Jupiter, 45
    passage of Pluto, 46–8, 57
    passage of Saturn, 51–3, 54, 114–15,
      116, 117
    passage of Sun, 44, 45, 49, 117
    traits of those born under, 63–4, 77
    and United States, 44, 52
Capricorn, 80
    associations, 39, 77, 125
    passage of Jupiter, 143
    passage of Neptune, 37, 90, 97, 99
    passage of Pluto, 36, 39–43, 47–8, 125,
      126, 143, 144
    passage of Saturn, 40, 90, 143
    passage of Sun, 65, 76–7
    passage of Uranus, 90
    traits of those born under, 40, 66, 77
    US Federal Reserve, 76–7
care centres, 99
Catholic Church, 37
Cézanne, Paul, 112
Challenger disaster, 87
charities, 58, 103
Chernobyl, 87
child labour, 52
Child, Lawrence, 122
China
    Cultural Revolution, 86, 127
    emerging market, 18
    wars and tensions, 84, 87, 90, 92
Chiron
    credit bubble, 71, 74
    and Jupiter, 125–6, 128–9
    and Neptune, 74, 125–6, 128–9, 133–4
    and Saturn, 54, 74
    stock market activity, 119, 125–6,
      128–9, 133–4
    and Uranus, 74
chocolate, 21
Churchill, Winston, 7
Cisco, 27
Clinton, Bill, 82
cocaine, 102
cold fusion, 91, 94, 102

Colombia, 73
Columbus, Christopher, 19
comets, 3, 15, 122
communism, collapse of, 9
community affiliations, 107
computer viruses, 29
concentration camps, 83
construction industry, 108, 114, 132
cooperative shopping movements, 107
copper, 75, 112–13
corruption, 37, 55, 68–9, 78
    accusations against US President, 57
    information networks, 64
    potential for, 20, 71, 106
    through misinformation, 20, 22
    World Bank, 39
cosmic collisions, 5
cosmic debris, 5
cosmic defence shield, 5
craftsmanship, 118, 138
creative accountancy, 23, 38, 50, 67, 72
credit bubbles, 60, 71, 74–5, 76, 128, 142
credit cards, 123, 141
credit facilities, 113–14
Crick, Francis, 133
currency crises, 32–3, 55–6, 76–8
    counterfeit, 73–4
    global currency, 110, 122
    price movements, 75
    significance of US dollar, 74–5

Dambusters, 4
dams, building of, 67–8
de Gaulle, Charles, 90
de Silhoutte, Étienne, 122
debt, 71–2
    between generations, 40, 60
    changing individual attitudes, 141
    dot-coms, 28
    and drugs, 73
    global levels, 28, 32, 40, 60, 67, 69, 74
    and IMF, 69
    Neptune, 71, 72, 74
    Pluto, 71, 72, 74
    Saturn, 114
    to the World Bank, 61
    US national, 56, 59
    wiping out of, 136
Degas, Edgar, 112
Delibes, Léo, 112
Denmark, 83

Index

depression, 99
derivatives, 28, 141
designer babies, 106
dinosaurs, 4
diseases, 84, 91, 100, 101, 102,
    105
DNA, 133
Dominican Republic, 86
Doppler, Christian, 100
'dot-coms', 26, 27, 28–9, 30, 38
Dove, Heinrich, 100
Dow-Jones index, 26–7, 113
down-sizing, 42, 125, 127, 129
dreams, 94–5
drugs industry, 26, 72–3, 99, 103, 133
Dvořák, Antonin, 112

East India companies, 21
Eastern cycle, 17–18
Egypt
    nationalism, 90
    pyramids, 12, 145
Einstein, Albert, 94
Elliott cycle, 27
Enron, 27, 38, 50, 54, 74
environmental conditions, 102
environmental groups, 67
environmental impact, IMF policies, 61, 67,
    69
epidemiology, 102
Ericsson, 30
ether, 101
Euro currency, 32–3, 76, 122, 123
experiments, 1

Fair Deal, 52
Falkland Islands, 51, 82
families, role of, 42–3
Faraday, Michael, 100, 106
fashion industry, 118
financial services, 23, 121
Finland, 83
floods, 4, 81, 116
food industry, 114, 116–17
food preservation, 21
Ford, Gerald, 49, 52, 53, 57, 58
Formalhaut, 16
France, 90, 122
fraud, 50, 68, 71
FTSE index, 113, 117

Galactic Centre
    founding of IMF, 65
    and Jupiter, 29–30
    and Pluto, 57–8, 59, 121–2, 144
    and Sagittarius, 65
    and Saturn, 29, 115, 140
    and Venus, 32, 112
gambling industries, 120–1
Gemini
    associations, 18–19, 30, 71
    passage of Jupiter, 30
    passage of Neptune, 18–23, 71
    passage of Pluto, 18–23, 71
    passage of Saturn, 30, 31, 117
geomagnetic field, 25, 62
Germany, 90
GM products, 117
gold
    association with Leo, 75
    as global currency, 74
    no known birth chart, 75
    US Federal Reserve, 78
gold prices, 78–9, 115, 123, 132, 136
    and Venus, 76, 79, 112, 113, 137
Goodyear, Charles, 100
Gore, Al, 49
government bonds, 39–40
Grand Mutation, 143, 144
Grant, Ulysees S., 27
Greenspan, Alan, 78
Grieg, Edvard, 112

Haiti, 87
Halley's comet, 122
Harding, Warren Gamaliel, 57
Harvey, Charles, 33
Hastings, Battle of, 3, 15–16
Haydn, Franz Joseph, 111–12
healing, 101–2, 134
Heckel, Johann Adam, 99
Hiroshima, 16, 85
Hitler, Adolf, 7, 83
home entertainment systems, 98
honour, codes of, 60
hospitals, 99, 101
housing markets, 40–1, 42, 108
human genome, 94

Icarus, 45
imagination, 94–103
IMF *see* International Monetary Fund (IMF)

Index

India
    irrigation projects, 68
    wars and tensions, 83, 86, 87, 92
Indonesia
    emerging market, 18
    tensions, 83, 87, 92–3
industrial sabotage, 20, 31
information
    developments in, 129
    and Gemini, 19
    see also Internet
insurance industry, 26, 97, 121
International Monetary Fund (IMF), 61, 63,
    65–70, 77
Internet
    future political role, 59, 98
    information availability, 1, 26
    information trading, 20, 71, 97–8
    and Neptune, 26, 97–8
    see also 'dot-coms'
Internet banking, 117
intuitive technologies, 101, 107
Iran, 87
Iraq, 48, 51
iris technology, 101, 107
iron and steel industries, 109
irrigation, 67–8
Israel, 82, 83
Italy, 73
Jackson, Andrew, 56–7
Japan, mortgages, 40, 60
jewels, 74, 112, 120, 137
Johnson, Lyndon, 86
Juglar cycle, 27, 28
Jupiter
    ancients' awareness of, 14
    Aries point, 135–6
    associations, 135
    Bretton Woods conference, 64–5
    Centre of Mass of solar system, 127
    and Chiron, 125–6, 128–9
    conjunction with Sun, 45, 47
    and Galactic Centre, 29–30
    and Mars, 132–3
    and Neptune, 125–6, 128–9
    passage through Cancer, 45
    passage through Capricorn, 143
    passage through Gemini, 30
    passage through Libra, 118
    passage through Taurus, 132
    and Pluto, 132–3, 139, 143–4

and Saturn, 28–9, 33–4, 89–90, 110,
    132, 140–3
and Star of Bethlehem, 4
stock market activity, 28–30, 118,
    125–6, 128–9, 132–3, 135–6, 139,
    140–4
technological breakthroughs, 91
and Uranus, 91
wars and tensions, 89–90

Kashmir, 83, 86
Kelvin scale, 102
Kennedy, John F., 49
Krondatieff cycle, 27

Landscheit, Theodor, 127
Lazarus, Emma, 44–5
Leibnitz, Gottfried Wilhelm, 106
leisure sectors, 112, 118, 120, 132
Leo
    associations, 64, 75
    Bretton Woods conference, 63, 64–5
    currency price movements, 75
    passage of Saturn, 120
    traits of those born under, 64
Libra, 80, 89
    Jupiter-Saturn conjunction, 141
    passage of Jupiter, 118
    passage of Sun, 115, 118
Lindbergh, Charles, 114
Lisbon earthquake, 88
Lloyds of London, 25
Long, Crawford, 100
'love bug' computer virus, 29
lunar eclipses
    Bretton Woods conference, 62, 63
    stock market activity, 119, 120, 127,
        130
    wars and tensions, 84, 129
lunar phases, 4, 55, 95, 124

magnetic storms, 3
magnetic therapy, 5
Manet, Edouard, 112
Mao Tse Tung, 7, 86
Mars
    ancients' awareness of, 14
    Bretton Woods conference, 64
    and Jupiter, 132–3
    and Mercury, 139
    and Neptune, 131

Index

Mars (*continued*)
 passage through Scorpio, 115–16, 131
 passage through Virgo, 64
 and Pluto, 53, 84, 132–3
 Presidential challenges, 53
 Presidential inaugurations, 50
 and Saturn, 84
 stock market activity, 115–16, 120, 127,
  131, 132–3, 139
 and Venus, 131
 wars and tensions, 84, 129
Marx, Karl, 85
Maunder Minimum, 8
media industries, 25, 31, 97, 113
medical developments, 101–2, 129, 133
medical research, sunspot activity, 7
mental health, 99, 100, 133
Mercury
 ancients' awareness of, 14
 Bretton Woods conference, 64–5
 conjunction with Sun, 75
 currency crisis, 76
 currency price movements, 75
 and Mars, 139
 and Neptune, 69
 stock market activity, 116, 139
 and the Sun, 138
mergers, 118
mesons, 109–10
metals, 109, 112–13, 120, 136, 137
 see also copper; gold
meteors, 5
Microsoft, 27
Middle East, 80, 81–2, 83, 84, 87
military hardware, 108
Mintaka, 145
misinformation, 19, 20, 22, 97
mobile phones, 30, 100, 101, 106, 113
Monet, Claude, 112
monoliths, positioning of, 12
Monteverdi, Claudio, 111
Moon
 economic stress, 55
 links with other planets, 17
 neap tides, 81, 124
 people born under Cancer, 64
 see also lunar eclipses; lunar phases
Moore, Michael, 98
Morse, Samuel, 100
mortgages, 40, 60, 141
Mozart, Wolfgang Amadeus, 111

Mundane Astrology, 33
music, 99, 111–12, 134

Nagasaki, 16, 21
NASDAQ, 28
nationalism, 90, 144–5
Nepal, 92
Neptune
 affiliation to Pisces, 26, 72, 97
 ancients' awareness of, 96
 and the arts, 98–9
 associations, 26, 50, 72, 90, 96, 97, 116
 Bretton Woods conference, 66
 and Chiron, 74, 125–6, 128–9, 133–4
 conjunction with Sun, 49–50
 creative accountancy, 50, 67, 72
 debt and credit, 71, 72, 74
 discovery of, 15, 96
 drugs, 26, 72, 73, 99, 103
 human imagination, 94–103
 and IMF, 67–8, 69
 and Internet, 26, 97–8
 intuitive technologies, 101
 and Jupiter, 125–6, 128–9
 and Mars, 131
 and Mercury, 69
 passage through Aquarius, 74, 95–6,
  98–9, 100–1
 passage through Aries, 96
 passage through Capricorn, 37, 90, 97,
  99
 passage through Gemini, 18–23, 71
 passage through Pisces, 74, 96, 97, 98,
  99, 100, 101–2, 103, 133–4
 passage through Sagittarius, 97
 passage through Taurus, 18
 and Pluto, 17, 18, 19, 20, 21–4, 35, 71,
  72, 73, 75, 123, 142
 Presidential inaugurations, 49–50
 and Saturn, 67, 68, 123
 scientific/technical developments, 100–3
 stock market activity, 25–7, 116, 125–6,
  128–9, 131, 133–4, 142
 traits of those born under, 67
 and Uranus, 99–100, 106
 and Venus, 67
 wars and tensions, 90
 world trade, 18–24, 71
nervous system, 19
New York, Great Fire of, 56
news sources, 19

Index

Nigeria, 86, 93
nitro-glycerine, 101
Nixon, Richard, 52, 53, 54, 57, 83
Norton, Arthur P., 13
Norway, 83

oil, 91
    association with Neptune, 50, 102
    prices, 78
Orion's Belt, 145
Oslo Accord, 82
ozone layer, 5

Pakistan, 83, 86, 87, 92
Palestinians, 82
Paracelsus, 133
Paraguay, 84
Pasteur, Louis, 102
peace protests, 129
pensions, 24, 40, 58, 125, 128
perception, 14
pharmaceutical industry, 99
Pisces, 89
    affiliation to Neptune, 26, 72, 97
    associations, 72
    passage of Neptune, 74, 96, 97, 98, 99,
      100, 101–2, 103, 133–4
    passage of Sun, 48–9
    passage of Uranus, 104, 105–6,
      113–14
planet cycles
    stock market activity, 25–32, 55–7,
      111–45
    and world trade, 17–24, 71
Pluto, 35–43
    ancients' awareness of, 96
    associations, 16, 81
    collapse of Soviet Union, 33
    creative accountancy, 72
    debt and credit, 71, 72, 74
    discovery of, 15, 36
    drugs, 73
    economic stress, 55, 56, 57
    and Galactic Centre, 57–8, 59, 121–2,
      144
    and Jupiter, 132–3, 139, 143–4
    and Mars, 53, 84, 132–3
    and Neptune, 17, 18, 19, 20, 21–4, 35,
      71, 72, 73, 75, 123, 142
    passage through Aquarius, 36
    passage through Cancer, 46–8, 57

    passage through Capricorn, 36, 39–43,
      47–8, 125, 126, 143, 144
    passage through Gemini, 18–23, 71
    passage through Sagittarius, 36, 37–9,
      41, 43, 53, 107, 122
    passage through Scorpio, 36–7, 41, 91
    passage through Taurus, 18, 36, 91
    passage through Virgo, 64, 136
    Presidential challenges, 51, 53
    and Saturn, 31, 51, 81–5, 128, 143
    stock market activity, 31, 57, 116,
      121–2, 125, 126, 128, 132–3, 139,
      142, 143–4
    and United States, 43, 45–8, 51, 53, 55,
      56, 57–8, 59
    and Uranus, 85–8, 116, 130, 139
    US Federal Reserve, 57–8, 77–8
    wars and tensions, 81–8, 90
    world trade, 19, 20–4, 71
Poland, 90
Polaris, 13, 15
pollution, 80, 81, 140
printing, 19
property investment, 40–1, 114, 116
protection services, 38–9
psychotic illnesses, 99
pyramids, 12, 145

radiation, 100–1, 106
radio waves, 3, 7
railways, development of, 22, 26–7
refugee crises, 10
religion, 134, 135
    Eastern, 17
religious authorities, 37, 58
religious visitations, 103
Rembrandt, 111
Renoir, Jean, 112
retirement age, 24, 40
Reynolds, Joshua, 112
Rhodesia, 86
Rodin, Auguste, 112
Roosevelt, Theodor, 7, 52
Royal Exchange, 21
Rubens, Peter Paul, 111
Russia, 34, 82

Sagittarius
    associations, 31, 37, 38, 53, 97
    and Galactic Centre, 65
    passage of Neptune, 97

Index

Sagittarius (*continued*)
    passage of Pluto, 36, 37–9, 41, 43, 53, 107, 122
    passage of Saturn, 139
    traits of those born under, 37
Saint-Saëns, Camille, 112
Saturn
    ancients' awareness of, 14
    associations, 81, 90
    Bretton Woods conference, 64
    and Chiron, 54, 74
    conjunction with Sun, 56
    and Galactic Centre, 29, 115, 140
    and IMF, 67, 69
    and Jupiter, 28–9, 33–4, 89–90, 110, 132, 140–3
    and Mars, 84
    and Neptune, 67, 68, 123
    passage through Cancer, 51–3, 54, 114–15, 116, 117
    passage through Capricorn, 40, 90, 143
    passage through Gemini, 30, 31, 117
    passage through Leo, 120
    passage through Sagittarius, 139
    passage through Scorpio, 137
    and Pluto, 31, 51, 81–5, 128, 143
    Presidential challenges, 51–3, 54
    Presidential inaugurations, 49
    rings, 51–2, 85, 88, 106–7
    and Star of Bethlehem, 4
    stock market activity, 28–9, 30, 31, 114–15, 116, 117, 120, 128, 132, 137, 139–43
    and Uranus, 88–9, 140
    and Venus, 15, 92
    wars and tensions, 81–5, 88–90
Schwann, Theodor, 106
science and technology, 94, 100–3, 104–10, 138–9
scientific experiments, 1
Scorpio
    passage of Mars, 115–16, 131
    passage of Pluto, 36–7, 41, 91
    passage of Saturn, 137
    passage of Venus, 116, 127, 131, 137
    stock market activity, 115–16, 119, 127, 131, 137
    traits of those born under, 36
security systems, 38–9, 42, 114
Sedgwick, Phillip, 62
September 11 terrorist attack, 31, 50

service industries, 105, 118
sewer systems, 41
shipping industry, 26, 38
Sicily, 73
Sierra Leone, slavery, 21
Simon, John, 102
Sirius, 16, 61
Sisley, Alfred, 112
slavery, 21
smart card financial management, 141
Smetana, Bedřich, 112
social change, 9, 10, 69, 140
socialism, 123
solar eclipses
    Bretton Woods conference, 61–2, 63, 66
    by Venus, 111–13, 137
    currency crisis, 76
    currency price movements, 75
    founding of IMF, 65–6, 69
    stock market activity, 115, 121–2, 123, 127, 130, 131–3, 134, 137, 139, 142, 144
    wars and tensions, 91–3
solar flares, 6
solar winds, 5
Sousa, J. Philip, 111
South Africa, 87, 90
South Sea Bubble, 22
Soviet Union, 83
    collapse of, 33, 90
space exploration, 86, 91
Sporer, Gustav, 9
Star of Bethlehem, 3–4
star-wars laser weapons, 106
stars, 12–16
    see also Sun
steam technology, 26
stock markets
    banking industry, 114–15, 117, 121, 123, 129, 130–1, 132, 137
    Chiron, 119, 125–6, 128–9, 133–4
    investment in arts, 111–12
    Jupiter, 28–30, 118, 125–6, 128–9, 132–3, 135–6, 139, 140–4
    lunar eclipses, 119, 120, 127, 130
    lunar phases, 55, 124
    Mars, 115–16, 120, 127, 131, 132–3, 139
    Mercury, 116, 139
    Neptune, 25–7, 116, 125–6, 128–9, 131, 133–4, 142

Index

stock markets (*continued*)
planetary cycles, 25–32, 55–7, 111–45
Pluto, 31, 57, 116, 121–2, 125, 126, 128, 132–3, 139, 142, 143–4
Saturn, 28–9, 30, 31, 114–15, 116, 117, 120, 128, 132, 137, 139–43
Scorpio, 115–16, 119, 127, 131, 137
solar eclipses, 115, 121–2, 123, 127, 130, 131–3, 134, 137, 139, 142, 144
sunspot activity, 7, 8, 11, 55, 119, 120, 124, 128
telecommunications industry, 30, 31, 113, 114, 117, 118, 119, 123, 132
travel industry, 39, 117, 123, 129, 132, 139–40
Uranus, 25–7, 113–14, 116, 136, 137, 139, 142
Venus, 32–3, 112–13, 116, 118, 120, 127, 137
strikes, 118
Sun, 2–3, 4–6
Aries point, 139
conjunction with Jupiter, 45, 47
conjunction with Mercury, 75
conjunction with Neptune, 49–50
conjunction with Saturn, 56
currency price movements, 75
founding of IMF, 65
links with other planets, 17
and Mercury, 138
passage through Aquarius, 49
passage through Cancer, 44, 45, 49, 117
passage through Capricorn, 65, 76–7
passage through Libra, 115, 118
passage through Pisces, 48–9
US Federal Reserve, 76–7
and Venus, 138
see also solar eclipses
sunspots, 6–9
Bretton Woods conference, 61
"double top" phenomenon, 8
human creativity, 101
stock market activity, 7, 8, 11, 55, 119, 120, 124, 128
Syria, 83

Table Bay, 21
Taiwan, 84
take-overs, 118, 137–8
tarot cards, 1

Taurus
associations, 132
passage of Jupiter, 132
passage of Neptune, 18
passage of Pluto, 18, 36, 91
passage of Uranus, 104, 109, 110
solar eclipse, 137
taxation, 41, 125
telecommunications industry, 38
stock market activity, 30, 31, 113, 114, 117, 118, 119, 123, 132
television, 98, 101, 109, 114
television stations, 58
temperature scales, 102
terrorism, 31, 38, 50
thalidomide, 133
Thames Barrier, 81
Thatcher, Margaret, 7, 51
theatre, 112, 120
thermodynamics, 102
tides, 55, 81, 96, 124
trade, and planet cycles, 17–24, 71
trance experiences, 103
transport industries, 109, 110
see also airline industry
travel industry, 109, 110
association with Sagittarius, 31, 38
stock market activity, 39, 117, 123, 129, 132, 139–40
terrorism, 42
Truman, Harry S., 49, 52
Tulipmania, 22
twin towers terrorist attack, 31, 50

United Kingdom
astrological chart, 116
housing market, 41
nationalism, 90
United Nations, 10, 58, 144
United States
as Cancer nation, 44, 52
civil tensions, 86
Declaration of Independence, 44, 45, 46
economic stress, 54–7
Fair Deal, 52
forecast of collapse of, 33–4, 44–59, 135, 138
housing market, 41
Independence Day celebrations, 44
and Pluto, 43, 45–8, 51, 53, 55, 56, 57–8, 59

Index

United States (*continued*)
    Presidential challenges, 51–4
    Presidential inaugurations, 48–51
    US Federal Reserve, 57–9, 76–8, 79
universities, 37–8
Uranus
    ancients' awareness of, 96
    Aries point, 136
    associations, 15, 26, 104, 114
    and Chiron, 74
    and Jupiter, 91
    and Neptune, 99–100, 106
    passage through Aquarius, 94, 105
    passage through Aries, 104, 106,
      107–10
    passage through Capricorn, 90
    passage through Pisces, 104, 105–6,
      113–14
    passage through Taurus, 104, 109, 110
    passage through Virgo, 64, 136
    and Pluto, 85–8, 116, 130, 139
    rings, 85, 106–7
    and Saturn, 88–9, 140
    scientific/technical developments, 94,
      100, 104–10
    stock market activity, 25–7, 113–14,
      116, 136, 137, 139, 142
    technological breakthroughs, 91
    wars and tensions, 85–9, 90

Van Dyck, Sir Anthony, 111
Velazquez, Diego de Silva, 111
Venus
    ancients' awareness of, 14
    associations, 65, 75, 112
    currency price movements, 75

eclipse of the Sun, 111–13
    and Galactic Centre, 32, 112
    gold prices, 76, 79, 112, 113, 137
    and IMF, 65, 67
    and Mars, 131
    and Neptune, 67
    passage through Scorpio, 116, 127, 131,
      137
    and Saturn, 15, 92
    solar eclipses, 111–13, 137
    and Star of Bethlehem, 4
    stock market activity, 32–3, 112–13,
      116, 118, 120, 127, 137
    and the Sun, 138
video mobile phones, 101
Vietnam, 53, 86, 127
Virgo, 64, 86, 89, 136

Wall Street Crash (1929), 137
wars and tensions, 80–93, 129
waste management, 41
water resources, 41–2, 67–8, 81, 91
weapons of mass destruction, 87
weather patterns, changes in, 9–10, 41,
    116–17
Western cycle, 17–18
Whittle, Sir Frank, 109
William the Conqueror, 15–16
Wilson, Woodrow, 52, 126
workers' rights, 52, 125
World Bank, 39, 61, 67, 68, 77, 78
world trade, and planet cycles, 17–24, 71
WorldCom, 27, 38, 50, 54, 74

Yamomoto, Commander, 47
yuppies, 28, 141